THE WORLD'S LEADING REAL ESTATE EXPERTS
REVEAL PROVEN PRICE STRATEGIES

·SO YOU CAN GET·

TOP
DOLLAR

FOR YOUR HOME

In Minimum Time!

Published by CelebrityPress®, Orlando, FL.

CelebrityPress® is a registered trademark.

Printed in the United States of America.

ISBN: 978-0-9907064-9-6
LCCN: 2015936124

This publication is designed to provide accurate and authoritative information with regard to the subject matter covered. It is sold with the understanding that the publisher is not engaged in rendering legal, accounting, or other professional advice. If legal advice or other expert assistance is required, the services of a competent professional should be sought. The opinions expressed by the authors in this book are not endorsed by Celebrity Press® and are the sole responsibility of the authors rendering the opinion.

Most CelebrityPress® titles are available at special quantity discounts for bulk purchases for sales promotions, premiums, fundraising, and educational use. Special versions or book excerpts can also be created to fit specific needs.

For more information, please write:
CelebrityPress®
520 N. Orlando Ave, #2
Winter Park, FL 32789
or call 1.877.261.4930

Visit us online at: www.CelebrityPressPublishing.com

THE WORLD'S LEADING REAL ESTATE EXPERTS
REVEAL PROVEN PRICE STRATEGIES

·SO YOU CAN GET·

TOP DOLLAR

FOR YOUR HOME

In Minimum Time!

CELEBRITY PRESS®
Winter Park, Florida

CONTENTS

FOREWORD

BY STEVE HARNEY

I've been in the real estate business for over thirty years. I ran my own 500-agent real estate firm and my expertise in this field has been sought after from such respected media outlets as *U.S. News and World Report,* the *Los Angeles Times* and the *Chicago Tribune.* Currently, I serve as the Founder and Chief Content Creator for *Keeping Current Matters,* a monthly informational presentation for top real estate professionals.

Now, I'm not telling you all this to brag – I just want you to understand that there's very little about the buying and selling of homes that I haven't been exposed to over the many years I've been in this business. That's why you may be shocked by the statement I'm about to make…

When I personally buy or sell a piece of property, I *always* hire a real estate professional to represent me.

Why would I need real estate agents when I know so much about the business? Simple. I know that they will negotiate better than I will – because I will be too emotionally invested in the outcome. For me, as it is for so many other homeowners, property is the biggest financial asset that I will have to deal with in my lifetime. That can't help but create a high level of pressure – which, in turn, could possibly cause me to make the absolute wrong decision on a transaction. That's why I hire professionals for my property deals – and I advise my friends and family members to do the same.

The right real estate agent will guide you through the five key aspects of any home sale:

1. Making sure you get the best price.

Of course, this is almost always a seller's top concern. As I just noted, a home is almost always your biggest financial asset. That's why you most certainly want to gain the most from that investment. Too often, however, you might get too aggressive with pricing to make sure you gain the most – and end up scaring away prospective buyers. On the other hand, you might be too timid and "give away the store" by pricing your home too low to make sure it does sell. A real estate professional will find the appropriate middle ground.

2. Doing the transaction on your timetable.

A change in work location or a sudden personal issue may force you into selling your home more quickly than is usual. Or you just may want to wait to make a move if, say, you have school-age kids you don't want to pull out of class before the term ends. Whatever the case, most people selling their homes have a certain schedule they need to stick to – and real estate agents will take that into account in terms of the approach to putting your home on the market.

3. Getting it done with the least amount of hassle.

A home sale can often be complicated. Inspections can reveal problems that need to be addressed, buyers may have certain requests that must be met, and, of course, the actual paperwork involved can be completely overwhelming. A real estate professional will tackle all of the above and more, so you don't have to. You might still have to make some hard decisions, but you'll be able to make those decisions confidently when you have the informed opinion of your representative to lean on.

4. Being able to easily relocate to your next home.

Selling a home is, of course, only one half of the battle. Making sure at the end of the transaction that you have a new home to move into is the other half. If you're not careful, you could end up owning two homes

– and paying two mortgages – at the same time. Or you could end up without a place to live at all, if you haven't managed to close on a new house! A real estate professional can help you execute the right timing to create the best conditions for a smooth transition.

5. Making sure your house gets sold.

Does this sound too obvious? Well, sometimes, this most important of points gets lost in the shuffle. A novice or inexperienced agent – or even home sellers that represent themselves in a transaction – can unknowingly throw up roadblocks and obstacles that ultimately get in the way of an easy, profitable sale. That, of course, will upend the previous four key points and potentially raise havoc on the home seller's life plans. This is a case where "keeping your eye on the prize" is essential.

The real estate pros you're about to meet in this book, *Top Dollar: The World's Leading Real Estate Experts Reveal Proven Price Strategies So You Can Get Top Dollar for Your Home in Minimum Time!,* are exactly the kind of people who can not only handle the above five key aspects of a home sale – but are also people who have been taught by two of the top real estate agents in the world.

Jay Kinder and Michael Reese, the two guys who put this book together, have dedicated the last decade of their lives to training real estate professionals to help homeowners maximize the return from their property transactions. That training comes directly as a result of their overwhelming success in the real estate industry. They don't just pass on what they read in a book or what they heard at a seminar - instead, it all comes from where it should, "hands-on" experience in the field. That's why everything you're about to read is practical, real-world advice from people who are experts at what they do.

For the first time in many years, it's a good time to sell – especially if you're putting your home up on the block in order to move up to a better one. First of all, interest rates are low compared to historic norms. Those rates will not stay that way, they're bound to start heading back north again. Second of all, home prices are rising and will most likely continue to do so. That means, if you wait a year or two to buy a new home, you could find yourself paying more both on the down payment for the home as well as your mortgage installments.

If you're considering taking advantage of the current real estate climate – or even pondering a home sale in the next year or two - then this is the book you should be reading. In my opinion, you can learn the most from the best – and the agents providing the content in this book qualify for that ranking.

I hope you enjoy hearing from Jay, Mike and this talented group, and benefit from their knowledge and expertise. Follow the advice they give you – and you'll never have a problem realizing "Top Dollar" on your home sales.

CHAPTER 1

HOW TO TURN TOP DOLLAR INTO NET PROFIT —
THE SINGLE PAGE THAT WILL DETERMINE HOW MUCH EQUITY YOU WILL WALK AWAY WITH WHEN YOU SELL YOUR HOME

BY JAY KINDER,
NAEA CO-FOUNDER

Obviously, this book is focused on selling your home for top dollar. Why would you want to sell for top dollar? Because homes that sell at the top of the market usually sell faster and have less hassles throughout the closing process. "Why?" you ask. Because a home that has been prepared, priced and positioned correctly in the market will give the impression that it is a "good deal" when compared to the rest of the homes in the market. This means you have the opportunity to hit the trifecta, the hat trick, or the turkey – if you are a bowler, when it comes to selling your home and putting the most equity in your pocket at closing.

Tell me if this is accurate. After your home is sold, you want to look back and acknowledge that these three statements are true.

1. My home sold for the most amount of money.

2. My home sold in the time frame I wanted it to sell.

3. The process was smooth and there were no surprises along the way.

You would probably agree that looking back on your home sale, if you can affirm those three things, you would be pretty happy with the real estate agent that helped facilitate the sale of your home, right? Me too.

The number one frustration many homeowners have, but don't think about, is related to the third statement. We are going to remove this threat by understanding the most frustrating part of the home-selling process that could be financially devastating.

Net profit!

At the end of the day, this is the number you care about. "How much money do I walk away with after everything is said and done?" So how do you figure this number out? "Won't every agent prepare me a net sheet related to the home sale so I can see what all the costs related to the sale are?" you ask. Well yes and no.

Yes, actually, it is required by law in most states for the seller to receive an estimate of net proceeds prior to putting the home on the market, and with every written offer you receive.

For your convenience, I've shared a sample document at: www. kinderreese.com/sellernetsheet for you to download and review. I've also included a video walking you through each of the areas I'm about to discuss here so you can accurately determine your net proceeds yourself.

In nearly every situation, the home sellers that follow the guidelines in this book, that painstakingly lay out how to prepare, price and position your home in your market, end up selling homes faster and for the most money. You can also download our, *How to sell your home for up to 18% more* report while you are on our website at: www.kinderreese.com/sellformore.

Here are the three things you should watch out for, when reviewing your estimated proceeds.

First, review the tax prorations. In many cases this is going to be one of the largest items on the closing statement and, depending on closing date, the title company could collect up to 12 months worth of prorated taxes at closing. This comes as a shock to many homeowners, and many agents, in an effort to make the net proceeds look favorable, will neglect to include this on your net sheet. The good news is that if your taxes are up to date or paid out of your mortgage escrow account, you will get a refund of the remaining insurance and taxes that are withheld. This usually is a surprise check you get in the mail, 1-2 weeks after the closing, from your mortgage escrow withholdings. Be sure to double-check these figures at closing.

Second, be careful of what you agree to if paying a portion of the buyer's closing costs. Different loans require different loan closing costs to be paid by the seller. This is most common in FHA or VA loans. If you agree to pay any portion of the buyer's closing costs, always cap that number, i.e., "not to exceed $X." This will keep you from getting stuck paying lender fees or origination costs that are out of the ordinary.

Lastly, the biggest threat to your wallet is related to repairs. This is the biggest negotiating mistake that is made when an offer is presented, and should be factored into your estimate as well. The buyer's offer will most likely have an amount for repairs, and that amount can usually be any number you can dream of. I've seen it be anywhere between $500 and $10,000. This means that you, the seller, would be obligated during the inspection option period, for repairs up to that amount. If the home inspector finds issues exceeding that amount, you are officially out of contract and renegotiation begins. The buyer has the upper hand here. You already agreed to your best offer and now the buyer can come back and ask you to do more than you originally agreed. Ouch!

You should consider doing a sellers home inspection that you can use to attract a higher offer, instead of giving the buyer the upper hand in the negotiation. This method is not common practice for all real estate agents, so be sure to ask them to show you their process to avoid pitfalls, and help extract the most money from your home sale.

About Jay and Michael

Jay Kinder

More than 10 years ago, Jay Kinder and Michael Reese inadvertently caught up with each other one summer afternoon at Lake Texoma. Real estate was the discussion of the day as a young Jay Kinder shared how he sold 233 homes the previous year to a very open-minded Michael Reese. Who knew that a chance encounter would turn into the wildly successful partnership that is now Kinder Reese Real Estate Advisors?

Michael Reese

Since that day, Michael, Jay and their teams have sold more than 4,250 homes combined. Together, they've brought in more than $18,000,000 in commissions for their real estate businesses, and haven't looked back since that fateful day.

Both Jay and Michael have been members of Realtor Magazine's prestigious "30 under 30" group. They have also both been ranked within the Top 100 of the 400 most successful real estate teams in North America by Real Trends of *The Wall Street Journal*.

Individually, Jay has established himself as one of the top agents in the world, selling more than 3,000 homes while capturing 14% market share in Lawton, Oklahoma. In 2007, Jay was named #2 in the World for Coldwell Banker, competing with over 120,000 realtors – being the youngest to ever obtain this achievement. The results don't stop there. In 2007, Jay was also ranked #1 in Oklahoma and #2 in the Southern Region including over 1,700 realtors from 14 states. He has been recognized with the honor of #1 Sales Associate in Oklahoma in 2002-2010 before opening his new company, Jay Kinder Real Estate Experts in 2011.

Michael has also enjoyed immense success as one of Keller Williams' top 50 agents worldwide. He is regularly ranked as one of the Top 5 teams in the Southwest Region for Keller Williams, and he and his team recently broke the record for buyer sales for the Keller Williams he worked out of in Frisco, Texas – before going independent as the Michael Reese Home Selling Team. Michael earned $1,000,000 in GCI after only his sixth year in the business and he's never made less since then.

In 2004, Jay and Michael started Kinder Reese Real Estate Partners with the aim of helping success-minded agents like themselves create the business and lifestyle that virtually every real estate agent dreams about. Kinder Reese currently serves more than 23,000 agents across North America with its revolutionary business model and innovative business systems.

In 2011, they co-founded the National Association of Expert Advisors® (NAEA), which offers the most prestigious designations that a real estate agent in today's market can have. The Certified Home Selling Advisor® designee has been recognized as an agent with a highly differentiated, proven, repeatable system to get sellers up to 18% more than the methods of average real estate agents. The NAEA's goal is to provide the highest level of education, training and business materials to agents who are truly serious about bringing the absolute best consumer experience to today's home sellers and buyers.

The Certified Home Selling Advisor® designation is a four-part certification process that helps today's real estate agents learn what they need to truly distinguish themselves from their competition and establish themselves as the true, number one choice for real estate consumers in their marketplace.

They are both best-selling authors on Amazon's top ten list of books for small businesses with their book *Trendsetters* and they can be seen on NBC, ABC, CBS, CNBC and other major networks as Expert Advisors™ on the television show, *The New Masters of Real Estate.*

Currently, Jay lives in Frisco, Texas with his wife Amber, and has three sons, Brayden, Karsen and Riggs. Michael lives in Frisco, Texas with his wife Stacey, and their two sons, Cache and Crew.

CHAPTER 2

THE POWER IN THE RIGHT PRICE

BY MICHAEL REESE

Your home is an investment and it should be treated that way. When it comes time to getting a return on that investment when you sell, pricing your home can perhaps be one of the most important tasks in that process.

Price it too high and your home sits on the market – losing you equity with each day that it goes unsold. Price it too low and you're leaving the proverbial money on the table. Most importantly though, the price of your home will help you create a home preparation budget and plan – to ensure that you get the most amount of money when it does sell.

The question is, how do you make sure you do the right things in the right order to price your home well enough, so you can walk away with the most amount of money for your home?

The answer is not as complicated as you might think.

One of the myths in the real estate industry is that homes sell for a fixed price. The truth is that homes actually sell in a range. Some of them sell at the top of the range and others sell at the bottom, which is even the case for homes that appear to be very similar on paper.

After spending more than a decade selling real estate and advising thousands of homeowners on what to do to get top dollar for their home, I've actually experienced the benefits of proactively managing the selling process so that homeowners were able to sell their home at the top of the range.

In fact, I've witnessed the exact same home, in the exact same area, selling for as much as 18% more than the other. The crazy thing is they both sold for list price.

There are logical reasons why some homes sell at the top of the market and others at the bottom. In this scenario, the reason the second home sold for less was because of the owners' motivation and reason: they simply priced the home low to get it sold.

The unfortunate part here was that the sellers' equity in the property was simply transferred to the new homeowner because after the home was appraised, it was worth 'way more' than what it sold for.

This should not surprise anyone; it happens every day. You see people buy homes, fix them up and sell them for more than they originally purchased them. In real estate, we refer to that process as flipping a home and it's something done regularly by real estate investors.

When investors buy homes, they determine what their budget is for fixing the home based on one variable: what the home will sell for once it's fixed. That simple equation determines if the home is a good investment or a bad investment and good investors know that all their decisions hinge on the price of the home.

THREE KEYS TO GETTING THE BEST PRICE

Like an investor, you need to make important decisions about the price of your home, which should ultimately come at the advice of an agent. Essentially, you need to be proactive in managing the process of selling of your home and have a home preparation and budget plan before you list. And, like any good real estate investor, you should make an educated decision on what you're going to do and how much you're going to spend to prepare your home for sale. That all starts by determining two things:

1) What your home would sell for if it were in optimal condition, and

2) What needs to be done to get it into that condition.

From my experience, there are three vital things a seller must do in order to ensure they get the most for their home: have the home staged prior to putting it on the market, get a pre-listing appraisal and conduct a pre-listing inspection prior to putting it on the market. The successful completion of these three activities virtually ensures that the home will not only be in optimal condition, but also that it will garner a price at the top of its selling range.

As well, there is one intangible benefit to proactively managing the sales process that is sometimes worth more than money, and that's peace of mind. Knowing what issues you're going to face ahead of time and being able to resolve them before they become a problem for the buyer can potentially save you a significant number of headaches along the way.

I. Staging the Home

Now, one of the critical points in the preparation process is to have your home staged by a professional home stager. By proactively managing this part of the process, you make your home shine in the eyes of the buyer because it's clean, well maintained and it looks sharp. Not only does it impact the price the buyer is willing to pay, it can also influence the appraisal price given on the home. A properly staged home can earn up to as much as 6% more than one that is just listed without being staged at all.

Knowing this, you'll want to have the home staged prior to the appraisal and before any marketing or collateral material is created. And, with almost 90% of home buyers starting their home search online, your first showings will likely start on the Internet. Having your home staged ahead of time ensures that the photos of your home are spectacular and give the buyer an excellent first look at what you have to offer.

Unfortunately, simply relying on negotiations to get top dollar is a reactive process that will likely net you less. By staging the home and putting it in optimal condition prior to sale, it will bring a higher price at listing time. From my experience, it takes way less negotiating skills to negotiate a high offer to top dollar than a low offer.

II. *Pre-listing Appraisal*

Most people know what an appraisal is because it was required by the lender to help protect their investment. Most appraisals are not ordered for the homeowners' benefit, they are ordered for the banks that are lending the money. It's their way of protecting their investment.

An appraisal by textbook definition is an "opinion of value." There are many techniques and choices appraisers have available at their disposal to support their opinion with facts. An appraiser has to have tangible proof in the form of comparable sales that meet Fannie Mae criteria for the purposes of comparison.

There is no required training on how to price a home for real estate agents. Most agents learn to do a CMA to help sellers come up with a price of their home, but the process is so varied and inconsistent across the board that it's not the most reliable means of determining price. This is proven by the fact that the bank uses an appraisal, and not a CMA, as a means of confirming the sales price for the loan.

In my experience, I've never met a homeowner who wanted to reduce the price of their home. I have, however, met many homeowners who have received terrible advice from agents that caused them to get less for their homes. Having a pre-listing appraisal is one way of treating the home as an investment and targeting the best price for your home. Plus, it requires a marginal investment on your part that helps you maximize the value of your home.

III. Pre-listing Inspection

A home inspection is a standard part of the home-buying process and unfortunately, it is the number one reason that a home sale falls apart. In addition to that, the home inspection is the part of the sales process where buyers and the agents who represent them seek to get further price reductions and additional concessions from the seller. It's also one of the greatest causes of headaches and stress for the homeowner.

To prevent all of these things from happening, I've had my sellers conduct a pre-listing inspection on their home. By doing this, the sellers have an opportunity to see what the buyer is going to see before the home goes on the market. As such, they have the ability to resolve any issues that the buyer might use against them in the negotiations.

Additionally, the seller saves a significant amount of money on any repairs that need to be done. Statistically speaking, the expense of having something repaired or replaced once the buyer discovers it during a home inspection can be as much as seven times what the seller would incur to resolve the issue. Most importantly, though, once the issues are resolved, the home is much closer to being in the best shape it can be to attract a higher offer and appraisal price.

What's even better is that the seller now has the inspection results – and proof of any repairs – to provide to prospective buyers to let them know that all the issues have been taken care of. This gives the buyer more peace of mind, confidence about the quality of the home and a better appreciation of the why the home is priced as it is. It also prevents the buyer from using the home inspection as a second negotiation on the price of the home.

At this point you might be asking yourself: "Is that all I have to do to get top dollar?" The answer, of course, is a "No." There are over 115 variables that must be proactively managed to help a seller navigate the home-selling process successfully.

That said, these three strategies – home staging, a pre-listing appraisal and a pre-listing inspection – are key elements in making sure that any home listed can justify selling for a price at the top of its range. The investment of time and money on your part is minimal, but the return you receive can mean thousands of dollars in your pocket when you receive top dollar for your home.

About Michael and Jay

Michael Reese

Jay Kinder

More than 10 years ago, Jay Kinder and Michael Reese inadvertently caught up with each other one summer afternoon at Lake Texoma. Real estate was the discussion of the day as a young Jay Kinder shared how he sold 233 homes the previous year to a very open-minded Michael Reese. Who knew that a chance encounter would turn into the wildly successful partnership that is now Kinder Reese Real Estate Advisors?

Since that day, Michael, Jay and their teams have sold more than 4,250 homes combined. Together, they've brought in more than $18,000,000 in commissions for their real estate businesses, and haven't looked back since that fateful day.

Both Jay and Michael have been members of Realtor Magazine's prestigious "30 under 30" group. They have also both been ranked within the Top 100 of the 400 most successful real estate teams in North America by Real Trends of *The Wall Street Journal.*

Individually, Jay has established himself as one of the top agents in the world, selling more than 3,000 homes while capturing 14% market share in Lawton, Oklahoma. In 2007, Jay was named #2 in the World for Coldwell Banker, competing with over 120,000 realtors – being the youngest to ever obtain this achievement. The results don't stop there. In 2007, Jay was also ranked #1 in Oklahoma and #2 in the Southern Region including over 1,700 realtors from 14 states. He has been recognized with the honor of #1 Sales Associate in Oklahoma in 2002-2010 before opening his new company, Jay Kinder Real Estate Experts in 2011.

Michael has also enjoyed immense success as one of Keller Williams' top 50 agents worldwide. He is regularly ranked as one of the Top 5 teams in the Southwest Region for Keller Williams, and he and his team recently broke the record for buyer sales for the Keller Williams he worked out of in Frisco, Texas – before going independent as the Michael Reese Home Selling Team.

Michael earned $1,000,000 in GCI after only his sixth year in the business and he's never made less since then.

In 2004, Jay and Michael started Kinder Reese Real Estate Partners with the aim of helping success-minded agents like themselves create the business and lifestyle that virtually every real estate agent dreams about. Kinder Reese currently serves more than 23,000 agents across North America with its revolutionary business model and innovative business systems.

In 2011, they co-founded the National Association of Expert Advisors® (NAEA), which offers the most prestigious designations that a real estate agent in today's market can have. The Certified Home Selling Advisor® designee has been recognized as an agent with a highly differentiated, proven, repeatable system to get sellers up to 18% more than the methods of average real estate agents. The NAEA's goal is to provide the highest level of education, training and business materials to agents who are truly serious about bringing the absolute best consumer experience to today's home sellers and buyers.

The Certified Home Selling Advisor® designation is a four-part certification process that helps today's real estate agents learn what they need to truly distinguish themselves from their competition and establish themselves as the true, number one choice for real estate consumers in their marketplace.

They are both best-selling authors on Amazon's Top Ten list of books for small businesses with their book *Trendsetters,* and they can be seen on NBC, ABC, CBS, CNBC and other major networks as Expert Advisors™ on the television show, *The New Masters of Real Estate.*

Currently, Jay lives in Frisco, Texas with his wife, Amber, and has three sons, Brayden, Karsen and Riggs. Michael lives in Frisco, Texas with his wife Stacey and their two sons, Cache and Crew.

CHAPTER 3

DISTINCT SERVICE AND PROVEN PRICING STRATEGIES

BY JOE DOMAN,
THE HIGHLY ACCREDITED REALTOR

As a Realtor, you want your clients to feel that their real estate transactions are smooth and assure them that they are working with a professional. However, there are many things that can happen, quite unexpectedly, despite your best efforts to thwart the outcome. As a PROFESSIONAL REALTOR, you know that **there is a lot going on behind the scenes** that clients may not realize, or even care about! Our clients' desire is to have a seamless transaction, first and foremost, and our goal is to make that happen. *We meet our clients' needs* by taking good care of everything that goes into their transaction, whether it's listing their property or finding them their next home. Through our personal codes of conduct, as well as our professional code, we hope to earn a satisfied client, and that is amazing! It's what keeps most of us in this business, isn't it? We love helping people and taking the uncertainty out of buying or selling a home.

Real estate is a people business. We deal with clients, other agents, banks, appraisers, inspectors, repairmen, front office contacts from various real estate offices and a slew of other

31

individuals. So much goes on behind the scene that is pivotal in making each transaction a journey that ends with a positive impression. *This is done through distinct service and mastering pricing strategies for your market.*

CREATING CLIENT CONFIDENCE

When I decided to make real estate my career ten plus years ago, I knew that I was going to seek out ways to make my clients feel at ease. *I wanted them to recognize the value I brought to their transaction.* A huge mistake many Realtors make is not explaining how we can help, which can make it difficult for clients to understand your value. A professional Realtor who understands the business as a whole, as well as specific aspects of it, is invaluable. I have always known I wanted to relay this value and I saw only one way to do this:

> *I needed to give my clients stellar service, provide value and it was imperative that I understand the pricing of my market and which strategies were best according to current market trends and buy/sell patterns. This would be best achieved through* showing *how I could help, not* telling *clients what I was doing. It wasn't my job to sell me; it was my job to market and sell the property. In turn, it worked out that clients wanted to work with me, because they knew I understood how to work for them.*

Realizing this was the breath that put life into my business. I began to brainstorm, taking advantage of ingenuity and the information that already existed. **I committed to finding a different way to look at the real estate transaction and pricing that would give buyers and sellers an advantage.** These ways would remain in compliance, obviously, but they did make a statement to my prospective clients and referrals. "This real estate game isn't what it used to be. This agent has a new and better way to do things."

Staying on top of the details when you reach a certain level of success in real estate is not always easy. Did you know that there are more than 15 people that touch each real estate transaction? Clients purchasing a home will talk to a few. Sellers of a home will talk with a few others. Eventually, after the details are in place, everyone attends a closing, which is where the money and keys exchange hands. It's up to my team and me to ensure that everything from start to close goes smoothly, and if there is a concern, we are proactive with it. *Yes, I do have a team—an amazing team—but as the lead agent, I hold myself accountable.* Real estate isn't a "pass the buck" business.

Here are five ways I have helped my team and myself conduct business in a *distinguishable* way:

1. We have two 120-point checklists for each property that we list. This helps us manage our clients' transactions behind the scenes. The first checklist comes into play when we start the listing process and it goes on until the home is under contract to be sold. The second checklist covers the time the house is under contract to be sold and goes until the day of closing.

2. We recognize that no two transactions are alike. There are different buyers and sellers, agents, backgrounds, purposes, and intent. This means that we **make no assumption(s)** and **take nothing for granted**. Doing this ensures that each transaction results in a client experience that understands that we were vested in his/her best interest.

3. We are problem solvers. When something comes up, we don't worry about why it came up and we dive right into solutions. Recently, I had a transaction where we were representing the seller side and were also representing them for their next purchase. *To our knowledge, everything was in place.* We went to closing and *surprise…the title search found a lien on the house*. It was from a previous owner, but this doesn't matter. Free and clear title is a requirement. To make matters tougher, the previous owners were on an

Alaskan cruise, which meant they were IMPOSSIBLE TO REACH.

The closing had to be postponed. Fortunately, due to creative solutions that worked for everyone's interests, we were able to close only two days later with an escrow for the lien amount. This was **great news** to report, because *the previous owners were not due back for 10 more days.* Ten days equals an eternity when you have everything lined up to sell your home and move into a new one. Without a proven record of being a Realtor that could be trusted, this likely could not have been accomplished.

4. *Create a team you can trust!* I'm blessed to have many members of my family working on my team, but there are others, too. **You must associate your real estate practice with people that are excited to lift the entire team up** and understand their role in the team. It's this cohesiveness that really adds distinction to your business in an industry that is very demanding and quite unforgiving.

5. *We've created a Buyers and Sellers Exclusive Advantage Program for our clients.* This is super exciting for us to roll out in conjunction with our Expert Advisor Home Buying/ Selling Systems. It's a fresh approach on creating value, and most importantly, it takes any uncertainty out of the buying and selling process for our clients. An example of how this benefits not only my team, but also our clients is:

We've identified over 100 different variables that can happen during a transaction. For our sellers/buyers, we help circumvent these variables, or save money on repairs if they become necessary, with our partnerships and various types of coverage we have in place. We provide our clients with Home Warranties, HVAC servicing, professional staging, video tours, Love it or Leave it program, utility concierge, appraisals, pre-inspections, house warming parties, and so on. They're all put in place to protect our clients.

Our data shows that we are able to get our clients anywhere from 10%-18% more for their listings when they list with us and that we save thousands for our buyers. This is something that we cannot claim without showing evidence to support it, and I truly believe it comes down to those five ways that my team sets ourselves apart in the very competitive real estate market.

YOUR PRICING STRATEGY MATTERS

Understanding how pricing works in your specific real estate market is essential to being an effective Realtor. You can be the nicest guy in the world, but if you cannot sell a home, you are not going to stay in business. Not understanding pricing will lead to few showings, fewer offers (if any), and a lot of time spent on a listing contract that you'll eventually lose. The right pricing strategy will depend on two primary variables:

(1). What your market is currently showing as favorable for buyers and sellers.

(2). What your client's goal or situation is.

Realtors who are able to stay in the business through all the "up cycles" and "down cycles" have seen many things and learned a lot. They are able to sustain because they understand what current market conditions are and how that impacts their clients. They also realize that their clients may have specific goals that they wish to achieve, such as either selling a home or buying a home or having a sell/buy combination. Some of the more common client goals may be:

- A quick sell due to relocation
- A quick sell due to financial duress
- Sell a current home and upgrade to a new home
- Sell a current home to downsize to a new home

You need to understand your clients' motives and guide them from there. Knowing how to price a home to help your sellers achieve their goals, regardless of what they are, is imperative.

FOUR PRICING STRATEGIES

Understanding the various pricing strategies out there is as important to clients as it is to Realtors. There are many, but the following are four that are common in my market and that I deal with on a daily basis. I do not recommend all of them, however, and I'll explain as they are discussed. Sometimes, what seems like a "good idea" is really a "deal-breaking" idea and knowing which is which has lent to my team's success. We close an average of 60 transactions per year. We're proud of that number because of the service we delivered while achieving it.

1) Overpricing

Overpricing usually happens because someone tries to sell their home on their own, or a Realtor is not committed to having a serious discussion about the possible implications of using this strategy. The main reason for this is that sellers feel it will leave them some "wiggle room." This is not a sound strategy, but it is not an uncommon one, either.

2) Rising Market (Upward Trending Markets)

This strategy is a targeted approach based on market research. What is happening in the market does not always reflect immediately in data or the media or with sellers. Here's an example of how this approach can be effective:

The market is showing an increase in housing prices, usually due to demand. You've done your research and you know this. You price the home about 2%-8% higher than where it may fall with just a basic market analysis. You market the home properly and you will get the offers. When the appraiser comes, make sure you go through the home with him/her and point out all the features and your numbers. After all, you know the home and the market well, and they are there for just a one hour appointment.

With rising markets you'll find that this can happen on its

own in a good market. You price the home well and know that it's in great condition from the pre-inspections, etc. One offer comes in and then another and eventually there is a lot of interest in that property, perhaps even a bidding war. Multiple offers draw the price of a home up. And these offers wouldn't be made if buyers in the market didn't have a need for the home that's being sold. This is a perfect example of the law of supply and demand. When inventory is low and there are a lot of buyers, prices go up.

3) Downward Trending Markets
A short sale is one where the bank takes lesser funds so a seller doesn't have to bring money into closing. Helping clients with short sales led me to formulate the following pricing strategy:

> *This pricing strategy prices the home below market value, as much as 5% or more, depending on the market you are in.*

When I first bring this option to clients, many of them feel panicked—until they hear what it is about. With this strategy, you are almost guaranteed to get multiple offers on a home, because both Realtors and clients understand a good price when they see it. Most often, by the end of negotiations, the price has gone back up that 5% (or whatever percentage under market you used), and, possibly, surpassed it. Everybody feels they got a great value: sellers want to get a great price and buyers want to get something at a good price, so the result is a win for everyone with this type of strategy

I've done 100 short sales to date, and this pricing strategy has worked every time. It further solidifies how having a system in place for pricing is a winning strategy.

4) Learning from comparables
Comparables are homes that have a similar appeal and are believed to have buyers with similar tastes and needs, as well. When you are listing a home, paying attention to the

37

comparables and what action (or lack of action) has taken place with them can help you create a winning formula for finding a price that moves. Here's a scenario that is based on a recent transaction:

Trying to find the best listing price, I found two comparables for basically identical homes. The overall price gap between the two was only about $5,000, but both of the homes had been on the market for 90+ days. We decided to list our home for $20,000 less than the one and $15,000 less than the other. The results were exceptional. We were under contract with 3-4 offers within 3 days and the price we were getting was higher than what we'd initially listed for. We got exactly what we were aiming for, and the house didn't have to sit on the market for an extended period of time. Without being aware of how to make comparables play to a seller's advantage, we could have been the third house sitting on the market for an extended period of time.

COLLECTIVE EXPERIENCE CREATES RESULTS

A curious mind and an adventurous spirit mark a successful Realtor. Look at what's out there and decide how you can distinguish yourself through your actions to be an advantage to your clients. Doing your research and homework will deliver results. Those results are what will set you apart from others and establish your team, or you individually, as a leader in your real estate community.

About Joe

With over ten years of dedicated real estate service, Joe Doman has become a leader in his market in the Ashburn/Brambleton, Virginia, area. He is a member of the National Association of Expert Advisors, as well as the North Virginia Association of Realtors, where he has been acknowledged as a Lifetime Top Producer. He and his team work for Re/Max Gateway in Brambleton, Virginia.

Being of the firm belief that continuing education and improvement are key contributors to real estate success, Joe is always eager to receive new certifications and increase his knowledge in all areas associated with real estate. His designations include: Certified Negotiation Expert (CNE), Accredited Buyer Resource (ABR), Certified Home Buying Advisor (CHBA), Short Sale Foreclosure Resource (SFR), Certified Distressed Property Expert (CDPE), Certified Home Selling Advisor (CHSA) and he has his GREEN designation.

It's Joe's attention to details and improvement that has made him a consistent, top producer. He began receiving acknowledgement for his excellence after only two years of being in the industry due to his commitment to providing distinguished service and his desire for expertise. Joe is also a member of the Re/Max Hall of Fame and the Chairman's Club since 2013.

Joe's adventurous spirit and love of being around people are two qualities that make him stand out to his clients, and to friends and associates as well. He gives his all to his clients and when he's not working, he gives his all to his family. Joe has four terrific children (Blake, Hadley, Elle and Brody) and one amazing wife, Miranda. His favorite hobbies include adventures in the woods with his son on their dirt bikes, getting a great work-out at the gym to feel good and keep the great ideas flowing, and being active in his children's lives and their interests and activities.

Joe believes that every day should be filled with commitment to what you cherish most, laughter and learning experiences. These qualities drive him to excel and are the reason that he is a highly-referred Realtor. To find out more about Joe Doman and the services he provides, visit his website at: www.JoeKnowsVA.com or contact him at 703-929-5716.

CHAPTER 4

THREE KEYS TO GETTING TOP DOLLAR FOR YOUR HOME

BY ANDREW LAMB

Meet Felix and Amy, owners of a beautiful two-story home in a desirable area of town. With prices rising rapidly, they realize they have quite a bit of equity in the property and begin the search for a real estate agent to help them determine exactly how much it's worth and to help with the sales process. The search, however, doesn't take very long. Why, you ask?

Let's face it, everyone has a friend or family member who sells real estate, either "full-time" or on nights and weekends after working another job. Since they are close to them and trust them implicitly with most other issues in life, they feel it would be a great idea to engage this person to sell their home. Unfortunately, what most home owners don't know is that **the average real estate agent only sells 4-6 homes each year, and 58.4% of the homes they list fail to sell.** I encounter these situations on a daily basis in my market in Northern California. You can imagine that a Realtor with less than a 50% success rate would be frustrated and desperate for a sale, yet **most uneducated homeowners are trusting the average frustrated agent to handle the largest financial decision of their lives.**

The above scenario is Felix and Amy's story. They listed their home with a friend that they knew was in real estate, and can you guess what happened? The home sat there... and sat there... and sat there. For three months they barely had any showings at all. Dismayed and embarrassed, they moved on to another friend in real estate to sell their home... and can you imagine what happened then? It sat there some more!

After the home failed to sell twice in 6 months, Felix and Amy had lost all hope that the house would ever sell, thinking that maybe the market had shifted or some detail about the home was putting off prospective buyers. They just couldn't put their finger on it. Little did they know that there was absolutely nothing wrong with their home... but there was definitely something wrong with their choice of real estate agent!

THE AVERAGE FRUSTRATED AGENT

You see, the average frustrated agent (AFA) only has up to 120 hours of formal training, spends less than $100 each month on marketing, and has absolutely no training or certification in marketing or negotiation. Due to this lack of training and experience, the AFA has a very short and simple approach to selling homes. His marketing technique consists solely of the three 'P's:

1. **Place a sign in the yard**

2. **Put the home in the MLS, and**

3. **Pray that a co-operating broker brings a buyer**

Although selling a home seems simple enough in theory, there are actually 115 variables involved in a real estate transaction, so it takes *much* more than these three activities to successfully sell a home in today's real estate market. I see situations like this far too often, and if you identify with Felix and Amy's story, I have good news! There is a better way to sell real estate.

ENTER THE CERTIFIED
HOME SELLING ADVISOR

If you want to sell your home in the least amount of time and for top dollar, you need a real estate expert who has a thorough and specific plan to get your home sold.

Fortunately, Felix and Amy found my company, The Lamb Team at RE/MAX Gold. With our 151-point marketing plan and our proactive Expert Advisor Home Selling Strategy, we sold their home in just two days and for more than the previous asking price... all without even having to put the home on the market! How did we do it? As a Certified Home Selling Advisor, I have a proven and repeatable system backed by market research to sell your home for up to 18% more money than the methods of traditional real estate agents. This Expert Advisor Home Selling Strategy includes a deep focus on buyer acquisition that allows us to preemptively have a pool of qualified buyers for a home *before* we list it.

Within this system, there are three keys to the successful sale of your home. Aligning your home selling strategy with these three keys will ensure that your home gets **top dollar** in the least amount of time possible in *any* market.

1. HIRE PROFESSIONALS TO POSITION
YOUR HOME PROPERLY

How a home appears online can determine whether or not that home actually sells, and how much the seller will net. A real estate agent who truly understands marketing knows that the first showing now takes place online. A 2014 study by the National Association of Realtors found that **92%** of homebuyers researched homes online. Furthermost, 43% of those homebuyers *started* their home search by looking online, and 50% did their research on their mobile devices. The Certified Home Selling Advisor understands that there are three elements that will determine whether or not a homebuyer actually takes the time to set an appointment to see the house in person: (i). the photos, (ii). the videos, and (iii). the decor.

Professional Photography

The old saying goes that a picture is worth a thousand words, but in real estate, a picture is worth a thousand dollars! In a day and age where modern technology allows us to take high definition photos with our smartphones, the AFA feels that it's perfectly acceptable to snap a few shots with his or her phone and upload them to the Multiple Listing Service. Little do they know that they are costing their clients thousands of dollars before negotiations even begin.

A Wall Street Journal article published by Emily Peck in October 2010 showed that homes with nicer listing photos taken with a Digital Single-Lens Reflex (DSLR) camera not only received more online attention, but they actually sold for up to $116,076 more than their competition whose photos were taken with point-and-shoot cameras and mobile phones. In spite of this fact, only 15% of all listings featured professional photography, including homes listed over $1,000,000.

A Certified Home Selling Advisor will insist that you bring in a professional photographer with a full-frame DSLR camera and a wide-angle lens. Ensuring that the photographer is skilled in High-Dynamic-Range (HDR) photography will provide a greater level of color and light balance to your photos, and will really make the home "pop" on screen. This all translates to added demand for your home and thousands of additional dollars on your net proceeds check.

Professional Videography

In addition to photography, hiring a videographer is a must when positioning your home to sell for top dollar. A 2011 study by Google found that **70%** of home shoppers toured the inside of a home through online videos. And where did they concentrate most of their viewing? YouTube! **YouTube is the top research**

tool used by homebuyers to conduct research on homes, more so than brokerage websites and other listing websites like Zillow and Trulia.

The Certified Home Selling Advisor knows that homebuyers are looking to video more than ever to fine tune their search and identify prospective homes (especially on their mobile devices). Working with a videographer who understands the intricacies of lighting, image stabilization and video editing will truly allow your home to shine in a competitive marketplace and sell for more money.

Professional Home Staging

The Certified Home Selling Advisor also has strong relationships with professional home stagers who can consult with you to ensure the home appeals to a wide range of buyers once on the market. Market research shows that homes that are staged sell in less than 30 days and for 6-10% more than homes that are not professionally staged.

Now, I know what you're thinking... "Won't these services cost me money?" The simple answer is yes - there is a cost to these services – but the relationship between your Certified Home Selling Advisor and these professionals will usually allow you access to these services at a reduced rate or even for free. The truth is that investing a few hundred dollars into preparing and positioning your home properly can mean the difference between the home sitting for months without a showing, or getting multiple offers in less than 30 days and selling for more than the asking price! Don't step over dollars to pick up pennies. Instead, invest in a proven process to get thousands of dollars in return. Professional photography, videography and home staging aren't just recommended; they are *essential* to getting your home sold for top dollar.

2. EXPOSE THE HOME TO AS MANY PEOPLE AS POSSIBLE

Exposing your home to the largest number of qualified buyers will get you the most money possible for your home. With this in mind, your real estate agent must have a clear and proven strategy to get your home in front of the right people at the right time for them to make a buying decision.

The Certified Home Selling Advisor has a comprehensive online marketing system. Some steps are as simple as having accounts with Zillow, Trulia, and Realtor.com, or as advanced as creating dark post advertisements on Facebook. True to its name, a "dark post" is a status update, link, or photo that is never published; it only surfaced as an ad that can be presented to an extremely targeted group of Facebook users. The Certified Home Selling Advisor will create an ideal homebuyer profile for your home and target them by geography, age, income range, profession, and/or interest. For example, if you are selling a high-end home on a golf course near a hospital, you may want to target doctors and nurses who work at that hospital and like to golf.

3. HAVE A SYSTEM IN PLACE TO RESPOND TO LEADS IMMEDIATELY

A recent MIT study noted that you have about 5 minutes to respond to a buyer inquiry, and failing to do so in that timeframe can reduce your chances of ever qualifying that lead by 21 times! The Certified Home Selling Advisor embraces this fact and has response systems in place to reply to each and every buyer inquiry immediately.

The Certified Home Selling Advisor's system for responding to and converting buyer leads includes:

- **Immediate Response Systems** that offer a live response in 5 minutes or less, 16 hours per day, 7 days per week, providing a connect rate that is 106x that offered by the average agent.

- **A Professionally Trained Sales Team** that is committed and held accountable to responding to buyer inquiries.

- **Lead Follow Up Systems** that have a Top 3 placement on Google, Yahoo and Bing to get the largest amount of buyer lead traffic handled the most efficiently.

- **A Buyer Loyalty Program** where more than 40% of the buyer business that comes in is from past clients and sphere of influence.

- **A Coming-Soon Listing Program** that gets buyers to seek out your listing and want access to your home while you're still preparing it for sale.

WHY LIST WITH THE EXPERT ADVISOR?

Abiding by the three keys within the Expert Advisor Home Selling Strategy will allow you to get top dollar for your home in any market. By establishing and running a successful buyer lead conversion system, the Certified Home Selling Advisor maintains a database of thousands of qualified home buyers to pre-market the home to for a quick sale. This is how I sold Felix and Amy's home so quickly. Studies by the National Association of Realtors show that homes that sell quickly also sell for more than the market average, so having access to a pre-existing database can allow you to sell your home to a ready, willing, and able buyer without ever having to list the home and deal with public showings.

Finally, having an Internet marketing and lead conversion strategy in place gives you the ability to showcase your home in front of thousands of buyers, not just the few who drive by and happen to see the sign. This means that instead of being listed as simply one of the hundreds or thousands of homes for sale in your city on Zillow, Trulia, or other listing syndication websites, your home will be prominently featured at the very top of the search results. This way, prospective buyers don't have to sort through page after page of home listings before seeing yours.

Couple this with proper positioning, and no one will be able to pass up your home online or otherwise.

About Andrew

Andrew Lamb is a native of Vacaville, CA and the founder and CEO of The Lamb Team at RE/MAX Gold. He holds a Bachelors of Arts in Linguistics from the University of California, Davis and is a Certified Expert Advisor, Certified Home Selling Advisor, and Certified Home Buying Advisor through the National Association of Expert Advisors.

Prior to his real estate career, Andrew owned and operated a digital marketing and strategy agency. When transitioning into real estate, his online marketing skills translated perfectly into the real estate industry of today, providing the knowledge and expertise necessary to help his clients maximize their equity position when buying or selling their home.

Over the last four years, Andrew has quickly grown his team of real estate experts to become one of the preeminent real estate companies in Northern California. Today, The Lamb Team at RE/MAX Gold is an organization dedicated to assisting clients with every aspect of the transaction through unmatched market knowledge and expert advice. For the price of one real estate agent, clients have access to individual experts skilled in selling, buying, marketing, customer service, outbound prospecting, negotiations, and handling your contract from start to finish.

Andrew's commitment to his clients and his business has earned him recognition as one of the most pioneering marketers and leaders in real estate. His innovative approach to sales and marketing has garnered attention from real estate agents all over the United States. With systems like his "Guaranteed Sale Program", "Certified Home", and "151 Point Marketing Plan", Andrew and his team of real estate experts can put up to 18% more money in your pocket than the methods of traditional real estate.

When not in the office, Andrew enjoys spending time with his wife Catherine and his two adorable little girls, Amani and Makayla. He also believes in giving back to the community, and has given countless hours to serving the under-resourced in his region through the Vacaville and Napa Storehouses and mentoring groups of young men in entrepreneurship and life.

For more information, visit his website: www.lambrealestate.com

CHAPTER 5

CHOOSING THE CORRECT REAL ESTATE AGENT

BY BEN JOHNSON

On my way to work early one morning last spring, I noticed that there were two homes newly up for sale in my neighborhood. One was listed with a well-respected real estate agent from the area. The other was listed as a FSBO (For Sale by Owner) using a local company that caters to the needs of owners who wish to sell their home without the help of an agent.

Both homes had great curb appeal, were in good repair, and of similar size. I assumed they would both sell quickly. Our neighborhood is in high demand because our school district is one of the best in the area. No one ever has trouble selling a home in this neighborhood.

I arrived at my office and pulled up the listings for each home online and immediately cringed. One of the homes was listed for a very reasonable price. The other home's price was awfully high – it was listed for $30k more than the first property. I looked for a possible explanation for the discrepancy – perhaps additional square footage in the basement – but found nothing. The first home was obviously listed at a price based on market data and the other was listed for what the homeowners hoped to get.

I was not at all surprised when the home listed by the agent sold within a month. It was beautifully staged and priced right. I heard that the homeowners even got more than they asked because they entertained competing bids.

The more expensive house, sadly, sat on the market for months before the owners pulled it and decided not to sell. The homeowners who listed FSBO didn't have all of the information they needed to be successful which led them to high expectations, incorrect preparation, and eventually, disappointment.

When I look back on my career as a real estate agent, I know I haven't "seen it all," but I have seen a lot. I've seen the real estate market during the best of times when new neighborhoods seemed to pop up overnight. I lived through the bursting of the housing bubble and the subsequent fallout. I've seen homes sell for much more than they were worth and I've seen homeowners take a loss because of bad financing and homes in disrepair. And I've learned that today, more than ever before, homeowners need a well-educated, real estate agent whose goal isn't just to help them manage offers and paperwork, but to get them the most from the sale of their property.

Homeowners who would like to sell their property are often overwhelmed as they try to find a starting point. Not only does it seem like there are a million little things to do around the house before you show it to prospective buyers; but there are so many questions about when to list, how much to ask, and so on. The most important thing a seller can do is to make sure that they work with a professional real estate agent who has solid experience. The sale of your home is a collaboration between you and your real estate agent, so make sure you choose the right partner.

Sellers lose a lot of money when they try to help out someone who is just beginning their real estate career. Maybe you've got a distant cousin who's new in the business and you want to give them an opportunity to prove themselves. But doing that is what sets you up to lose money. Of course, when this sort of thing happens it isn't because your cousin doesn't have your best interest in mind, but because they lack experience. Sometimes the issue is pricing, other times its negotiation, on occasion the problem might even be marketing. These are all parts of the process that are more important than most people realize.

So how do you find a professional who has experience? Here are a few key questions to ask any agent you are considering:

1. Ask how many homes they have sold. Experience comes from performing a task over and over again. The number of homes an agent has sold is often an indication of their familiarity with the process and their ability to effectively manage potential issues before they arise.

2. Ask your agent what their particular system for selling property is. What indicators do they use for pricing?

3. Ask any potential agent what they do annually with regard to their own education. In this industry things change constantly, and there is a wealth of information that can be acquired through classes and books.

A good real estate agent, someone who you want to work with, has experience, believes education is important, and is prepared to help you throughout the sales process. The first thing an agent should do is determine your needs. You are the one in the driver's seat and your agent is there to give you directions.

I know a young couple, Amy and Chris, who decided to sell their first home because they were starting a family. They'd spent four years remodeling their home. They'd taken it from a lackluster home on the block to something out of a magazine. When it was time to list the house, they reached out to one of the most respected real estate agents in their area. He was known for being one of the top-producing real estate agents and Amy was sure he would refer them on to someone with less experience.

To their surprise, he offered to come out and meet with them later that afternoon. He listened carefully to their stories about remodeling projects they'd completed. He walked through their home and all around the property with them, taking in every detail. He asked some questions and learned that it was important for them to move quickly because they had a house they hoped to buy. And to their surprise, he started representing them that very day.

Amy and Chris had a listing price in mind but he counseled them that a lower price was a better decision if they wanted the house to sell quickly. After some discussion they came to a compromise.

He set them up with a professional stager to help them put the finishing touches on their home. He came in with a trained photographer to ensure the photos would be of a professional quality and showcase the home when buyers viewed the listing online. And finally, he had them get a home inspection before they listed the house for sale. Doing so typically eliminates any potential surprises that a buyer's inspection may uncover. They followed his instructions and within a week, they had two competing offers. Today they have a family and are living in the home of their dreams.

When you are choosing your real estate agent you are creating a sales team. Remember that. You are creating a team with the goal of selling your house for as much as you can as quickly as you can. Because working as a team requires a dialogue, you should work with an agent you feel has your best interests in mind. You need to be open with them about your situation and reasons for selling you home – good and bad.

In order to give you the right direction agents need to know about your needs. If making the most money you can is at the top of your needs list and time is unimportant, you may want to wait until your garden is in full bloom or your landscaping will be in top form if that's a big selling point for your home. However, if the speed of your sale tops your needs list, you may need to price your home more aggressively in order to meet a deadline.

Your real estate agent should help guide you to your best options and help you make the right preparations. This would include things you can do to make more money on your sale, get a higher return, or even shorten the listing time period.

Painting and repairs are very common tasks when preparing to sell your home. I've known some very motivated sellers who decide to paint or replace faucets and rather than choosing neutral colors or more modern fixtures they choose their favorite colors and the cheapest faucets. This can end up hurting their ability to get what they want – whether that's speed or profit. Their intentions were good but they didn't have an expert's input to help them make the right choices.

A good agent should introduce you to professional stagers and photographers. With more potential buyers using the Internet to shop for their next home, it's more important than ever to have beautiful photographs of your home decorated and organized in a way that is appealing to buyers. It is a real turn-off for potential buyers to see a home that is too cluttered or too empty. If the photographs you supply are dark or out of focus, it's highly likely that a buyer will move right past your listing.

A note to consider about the Internet and its place in the real estate market. Buyers and sellers alike have access to a great deal of information about real estate online. Some of that information is good, some isn't. Using the Internet to get a sense for other homes currently on the market and how your home measures up is fine, but get an experienced agent's opinion as well. Let your agent give you their expert advice because, after all, that's one of the reasons you're paying them!

On occasion your agent may suggest getting an appraisal or inspection before determining your listing price. For example, if you live in an older home, it might be important to have inspections done before listing so that there are no surprises after you've agreed to price and terms with a buyer. Perhaps you have a highly unique home or it is decided that it is best to have a second opinion to substantiate the market value of your home. It may be the best stregy to get an expert appraisal completed before listing your home sale in an effort to reinforce the list price within the range of prices where your house falls.

An experienced agent - one who is working in your best interest - will also incorporate predictive modeling when determining when to list your property and how much to ask for it. Predictive modeling is one of the tools a real estate agent has at his or her disposal that can help homeowners get the most from the sale of their property. It allows agents to use data and analytics to help forecast the trends that will help you to sell your home. The data helps provide a snapshot that will help determine what to ask for your home, when to list it, how many similar homes are on the market and what buyer behavior looks like currently.

Predictive modeling is used in a myriad of industries – from information technology and meteorology to disaster recovery. No matter where it is being used it allows decision makers, in our case homeowners and real estate agents, to make choices that will help them be successful.

I live in Minnesota, so I know that listing your property in the winter is going to present certain challenges. During Minnesota winters, the real estate market slows down considerably because of the weather. But we can't assume that just because the weather is cold we will see fewer home sales or see homes selling for less. Some years the number of homes for sale is low. This is one piece of data that would indicate homeowners can expect to sell at a higher price. Predictive modeling helps us understand how home prices may change depending on factors like the weather and inventory. It helps agents to clearly understand the current market and take those conditions into consideration when we help homeowners.

When it comes to pricing a property there's always a range – a high and a low. It is important to take into account all of the variables so that you can be assured the listing price you choose falls within that range. Obviously, when a seller is able to be somewhat flexible, we want to position them in a way to capitalize on the market. This means using the information available and being aware of conditions that will positively or negatively affect the price of their home. This creates a strategy to sell their home for the best price possible. Often agents have access to premarket data that can tell us if a certain area is verging on high inventory levels. This is exactly the kind of data we want to consider when choosing the date and price to list your property.

Predictive modeling is a way to understand the big picture as it directly pertains to selling your home. An agent who understands predictive modeling can help predict the behavior of potential buyers and therefore help you to list your house at the right time and at the right price. In my opinion, all agents should be using this model to help the homeowners they work with, but many rely on much less information.

From time to time I work with expired listings – homes that were listed but never sold. This looks bad for the agent who was attempting to sell a home and the homeowner is often panicked that their home will never sell. When I have a conversation with the homeowner and review the situation, the most common issues were incorrect pricing, improper presentation of the home and little to no marketing. Often the issue that led to an expired listing was pretty simple – perhaps they were priced too high or the property wasn't marketed effectively. Often the agent was simply inexperienced or lacked a repeatable model for selling homes the right way.

Sellers quickly begin to understand just how important an experienced real estate agent is after something like this happens. When you work with an agent who sells 5 or 6 times the number of homes the average agent does, you reap the rewards of that experience. Obviously an agent who sells a significant number of homes is doing something different and something effective to produce those results.

Selling a home is a collaboration between the homeowner and their real estate agent. As a seller you need to think of yourself as part of a team. If you choose to collaborate with the right agent, one with years of experience and a reputation you can trust, you may rest assured that you will be receiving the right guidance and get the most out of the sale of your home.

About Ben

Ben Johnson is a well-respected realtor working in the Minneapolis area. Before he began his career in real estate, he worked for an architectural firm in San Diego that specialized in construction defect litigation. His experiences led him to an interest in real estate that eventually grew to a passion to learn all that he could.

In 2004, after relocating to the Twin Cities and obtaining his license, Ben focused on carving out a niche for himself in real estate. Over the last ten years, Ben has had experience with new construction condominiums and property resale and buyer representation (including bank-mediated sales). Ben has grown a very successful business based on his integrity, knowledge, and service.

In today's Twin Cities real estate market, finding the right real estate agent representation is crucial. Ben has real estate expertise to share and is adept at helping his clients prepare for the process of buying or selling a home. He is there to guide and inform you through every phase of the buying or selling process.

Ben works with homeowners in all areas of the Twin Cities metro area and has had the good fortune to work with multiple real estate developers as well. That experience has given him a firm grasp on the local market and the insight to make sure his clients are making an informed decision – whether they are buying or selling property.

Ben's knowledge of real estate, integrity, and attentiveness to his clients' needs set him apart. Ben was voted "Super Real Estate Agent" by *Mpls.St.Paul Magazine*, welcomed into The Masters Circle with Edina Realty, and ranked the #19 Individual Agent in Minnesota by Transaction Sides from Real Trends.

Here's what people are saying about him:

> *"Real estate agents all owe a lot to Ben for helping undo the stereotype. Ben is more guide than salesman, and my first impressions of him as such followed through the entire process. Recommend him? Sure. Nominate him to train his fellow brothers and sisters of the trade how it*

should be done? Absolutely." – Chad Calease, *client*

"I wish there were more of Ben in our office - intelligent, knowledgeable, ambitious, hard-working, professional, and most important for someone in sales, he's a 'helluva' nice guy. Ben doesn't wait to be helped, and doesn't come to work with a sense of entitlement - if he doesn't know it, he learns it - if he senses another opinion is in order, he seeks it - if it needs to be done, he does it." – Matt Loskota, *Broker at Edina Realty*

If you wish to buy or sell property in the Twin Cities metro area, don't hesitate to reach out to Ben Johnson. His integrity and commitment to service are two benefits you'll see when you choose him to help you buy or sell your home. You can reach Ben Johnson at Edina Realty by calling (612) 239-4858 or sending an email to: Ben@BenJohnsonGroup.com.

CHAPTER 6

HOW TO SUCCESSFULLY WORK WITH INTERNATIONAL CLIENTS

BY DIANA ZHUANG

UNDERSTANDING CULTURE IS THE KEY TO SUCCESSFULLY COMMUNICATING WITH INTERNATIONAL CLIENTS

As a first generation immigrant from China and an active real estate professional on the front lines for 18 years, I can clearly state: communication with crystal clear understanding of cultural differences is the key to working with international clients.

I came to the United States in the fall of 1992 to get my MBA. Before then, I had two highly respectable jobs—teaching at a university and as an engineer at a top research institute. When I just arrived in the United States, I felt the sky was so blue, the grass was a lovely green and even the moon in Texas seemed bigger than what I had seen in China. However, between the blue and green, I had to start my life here under difficult circumstances. I did not even know how to operate the drinking fountains here. I had to learn everything from scratch.

In 1997, I became a realtor. During contract negotiations, I noticed there were very different mindsets between Chinese and Americans, even among Chinese and American real estate professionals. While Americans would focus on monthly payments, the Chinese would focus on the purchase price. Some international clients did not notice that a 0.25 percent increase in the interest rate could increase the cost of purchasing a home in the $250,000 price range by around $10,000. Some international homeowners tried to cut their water bill by not running their sprinkler systems as often as they should, which caused foundation trouble. The foundation repair costs, plus the negative effect on their home's resale value, could be greater than the total of 8 years worth of water bills. I feel it is my obligation to use my knowledge to help everyone that I can, especially my clients. Not only to help them purchase, sell or make any kind of investment, but also to help them to make wise decisions . . . to reach their ultimate goal . . . to add value to their life. Meanwhile, my life will be more meaningful through my contribution to my clients and the society.

No matter how passionate you are, in order to succeed in working with international clients, you have to always pay special attention to the cultural influences.

I held an open house last year. There were more than 70 visitors that came within an hour. Ninety percent were of Indian descent. More than 60% of the visitors told me that they liked the home, but they wanted a home entry facing to the east—the direction of the rising sun. Only one Indian buyer presented an offer. The home quickly sold, but the buyer was not Indian.

If you are representing an Indian buyer client who must have an east-facing house, you'd better know how important it is. Otherwise, suppose, based on your limited knowledge, you recommend a home that represents the best value in his price range that requires modest remodeling. It is a dream home – except it is not facing the direction of sunrise. Instead, it is facing west. What may happen? The lovelier the home, the more pain the buyer may feel. The elegant kitchen with Verde bamboo granite counter top and most fashionable cabinets may hurt the buyer's feelings much like your pointing him to a mirage. The "dream home" can become a nightmare. If you keep ignoring your buyer's needs, the harder you work for this client, the more stress you place on his shoulders, and the further you push him away.

FOUR THINGS THAT CAN HELP YOU UNDERSTAND A CULTURE

Do we need to cross the world to know all of the different cultures first before conducting our business? No, it is impossible and illogical. There are four simple things that can help you to understand different cultures and lead you to success.

First: See beyond – What we see with our own eyes does not always tell the truth!

I worked with one client who was new to this country at that time. He was a handsome and brave man. One of the first things he learned upon arriving here was: smart Americans use other people's money to make money. So, he put his funds in the bank and paid all his bills by credit card. My duty was to find him a commercial building so he could start his retail business. His eagerness to succeed made him also eager to learn American culture. He told me: "Diana, I trust you. If you see anything that I do not do right, please correct me immediately."

The first lesson started with opening doors.

When we approached the entry of the building I was showing him, he walked in and let the door close right in front of me. I said to him, "Next time, please hold the door open for a lady." He did when we left the building, but he did not hold the door for the gentleman right behind me. I told him, "You should hold the door until the person behind me passes through the door – if he is very close to me."

The next day, we met a commercial listing agent in the parking lot. The agent was talking as he led us to the suite for lease. As we approached the entry, my client suddenly sped up, cutting in front of the other agent, almost tripping him. My client made a beeline for the door, he was on a mission. He opened the door; standing there, holding it with a smile on his face as bright as sunshine. A surprised look was on the face of the listing agent, but he held his composure like a true professional.

Suppose you meet an international client and on Day One, he let the door slam in your face. On Day Two he almost trips up the listing agent among other odd behaviors. How would you handle it? If you only trust your eyes, you may feel these behaviors were rude—embarrassing. But if you can see beyond, if you can see what may lie behind these behaviors, you may feel this client is very lovely and brave. Because he does not know what he does not know, he has realized that and challenged himself to fit in very bravely, so he will go through an awkward time period, but he will pass through it quickly and become very successful.

Second: Listen with your heart to hear what people have NOT told you!

One of my past clients introduced me to a new buyer client. The first time I met her was at a property she picked out. The BMW SUV she was driving indicated she was rich. When we entered the property, she hardly talked to me. She ignored most of my introductions about the property. Whenever we made eye contact, she quickly turned away, looking up at the ceiling. No trust, no respect, and absolutely not friendly. I was not very comfortable at that moment. Referrals are a significant source for my business and clients who come from referrals are normally my best clients. The trust was built before they met with me. Most of the time, the first appointment feels like meeting an old friend.

What was my client's body language telling me? What was the cause of her arrogant attitude toward me? I forced myself to ignore her attitude and try to hear what she had not told me. I stopped my introduction to the property and the surrounding community and went to simple questions:

- "Do you like the high ceilings?"
- "Have you seen anything you do not like?"

We started to talk to one another. When the conversation started, she asked a lot of questions that did not apply to our real estate market or were not realistic. What I gathered from these questions was that she was a very detailed, analytical person—smart and creative but with no basic knowledge about the common rules here. I gave answers with clear explanations for each of her questions. Before leaving, she had become so friendly. Later, I learned that she was a very successful businesswoman in China—rich and super smart. However, she had been mistreated by another Chinese agent before she met with me. Another agent felt she was stupid and treated her disrespectfully. So, this fact made me realize that even for people who share the same culture and language, "listening with your heart" is a big challenge.

I found her a home and we have become personal friends. The more I get to know her, the more amazing I feel she is. Up to now, I still enjoy her new stories when we meet. When we help our clients make decisions about one of their largest lifetime investments, listening is more important than talking. Listening from the heart is even more important than just listening.

Third: Do not make wrongful judgments if you see something strange.

Can you imagine arriving in a new country, not for a vacation, but to live there? What would you have to deal with? You need to find a hotel, but you do not know how. You need to buy milk, but you cannot drive. You have tons of questions, but you cannot speak English. No matter who you are or how successful you have been in your home country, you cannot really leverage too much from your previous experiences in your home country. You are a new born baby to this new world, but you have to manage it like an adult. The moment you landed in this new land, your life shifts—like dropping from the New Texas Giant at Six Flags Amusement Park.

Now you need to invest in a house or an apartment, but you have no credit history in the U.S. Unfortunately, in the real estate business, a lot of agents do not understand these factors. Many real estate "professionals" have mistreated these foreigners just because of their accent. The sweet voice can suddenly become cold. They assume the person on another side of the line is inferior.

If you want to work with international clients, you have to try to understand and respect them first. When you feel they cannot talk as politely as local people, they may be limited by their vocabulary. When they ask you too many questions, it may because they do not have basic common knowledge. When they ask you to help them to do something that may be wrong here, you should consider that it may be doable in their home country.

I worked with a group of Indonesians buyers. They are very nice people, and they all become my friends after closing. Most of them have become my repeat clients. A majority of them have one thing in common. They will be late for their appointment time, averaging about 10 minutes. I always keep a book inside my car; that will be my reading time. I will manage the showing time when I meet with them, so I will not cause any delay for my next appointment. If you cannot change their culture, then the best way is to deal with it is to make a good plan for it.

Sometimes it takes extra effort. The international buyer can pay cash to close a real estate transaction, but they may need your help to open utility services. If you are too busy to do it, outsource it or find a solution for it.

Fourth: Respect differences!

I worked with an overseas commercial investor. I arranged a meeting to show him an apartment. The moment I met with him, I felt surprised. His dress was way too casual—like he was going to the beach. And even for that environment, the shorts were cut too short. A day before, I told him that he could dress "business casual." Obviously, we had a different understanding of "business casual."

When we arrived at the apartment office, the owner and the manager were very polite, but I could tell that they were taken aback by my client's appearance when they looked at each other. The laughter in their eyes was very loud.

The investor did not realize what was going on inside the office. He was very direct in asking a few questions, some of the questions the owner would not normally disclose to buyer prospects before reaching a purchase agreement. His questions brought a surprise to the owner. However, because he was a cash buyer, the owner tried to cooperate and provided the cash flow sheet. The investor was not an English speaker and could not read the cash flow sheet. So, he asks directly: "What is your annual net income?" I translated the question and the manager said he needed to do some calculations. When the manager started to work at his computer, the investor simply asked me a few questions: "Diana, show me what is the gross income?" I pointed out the number to him. Then he asked me "What are the operating expenses?" and so on. When he stopped asking, he paused only for a moment, then he gave the net income number. He calculated it faster than the manager who was sitting in front of his computer. Then, everyone forgot about his funny dress as they realized that he was a sharp, capable investor.

The owner and the manager's attitude changed. When they were driving us around in the golf cart to show my client the complex, even my client was laughing and joking about things that do not make sense to an American, but he was treat like a professional investor buyer.

To work with international clients, real estate professionals need to get out of their comfort zone, see beyond the surface and be willing to go the extra mile. The deeper your level of understanding the culture, the more success you will gain.

About Diana

Diana Zhuang, Founder of Spark Realty Corporation, has been very active in the real estate industry for 18 years. While she manages a successful real estate brokerage in Texas, Diana has also become a successful real estate investor in single-family residential, multifamily commercial, land, performing and non-performing notes all over the United States.

As a first generation immigrant from P.R. of China, Diana has a deep understanding of how cultures and personal backgrounds can affect business decisions. She uses that understanding and her knowledge of different facets of the real estate industry to guide her international clients to successfully complete real estate transactions. Services offered include residential single-family home purchase and sale, commercial real estate, single-family residential, land and performing/non-performing notes investments. Due to Diana's high level of customer care and her extensive knowledge of the real estate industry, she consistently receives referrals from her clients. In fact, these referrals have become the foundation of Spark Realty Corporation's business.

Spark Realty Corporation's Mission

- To help our clients achieve their maximum level of success.

Spark Realty Corporation's Core Values

- Our Client's Best Interest Is Our Top Priority.
- Forming strong, mutually-beneficial network relationships with the best in the Real Estate industry.
- Focus on solutions and have a positive mindset.
- Continued improvement through investment in Technology and Education.

Spark Realty Corporation's Capabilities

Spark Realty Corporation is not a traditional real estate company. Spark Realty Corporation has networked with the most successful real estate agents, the best single-family and multifamily property investors and the most seasoned note investors from across the nation. Spark Realty has even networked with award-winning, internationally-acclaimed architectural design firms for clients interested in building large commercial projects. Leveraging these networks has provided Spark Realty Corporation clients to reap higher returns on their investments. Spark Realty Corporation can manage commercial projects from site selection to project completion.

Diana is a member of:

- National Association of Experts Advisors
- Lifestyles Unlimited, Preferred Investor
- Diamond Member of Note School
- National Association of Real Estate Brokers (NAREB)
- Asian-American Real Estate Association (AAREA)
- Greater Dallas Planning Council
- National Association Of Professional Women
- National Association of Realtors

To contact Diana Zhuang:
Diana@Spark-Realty.com
www.Spark-Realty.com

CHAPTER 7

SEVEN PROVEN LAWS TO HELP REACH THE TOP OF THE 22% PRICE SWING ... VIOLATE THEM AND PAY THE PRICE!

BY CURTIS JOHNSON

MORE EXPOSURE = MORE $ IN YOUR POCKET

The sun was just coming up as I stared out the window giving directions – take a right here ... now left ... there it is, on the corner. The game was on. There was a rush at each stop. Saving $10 on old baseball cards, a great chair for $20, or negotiating for a punching bag for $3. Huge victories!

Simple lessons on these Saturday mornings growing up would help my future clients selling their homes, and more importantly, help heal a broken relationship between a mother and son. I was a punk teenager and these were just simple garage sales in San Jose, California, right? What do they have to do with selling your home today?

71

There are a lot of ways to sell a home. There are very few ways to sell it fast, *and* for top dollar. I'll share seven key takeaways that I learned on the garage sale trail that have helped me sell well over 3,000 homes for "Top Dollar."

LAW 1 – CHOOSE YOUR STRATEGY

You're at a fork in the road. Do you go left or right? High or low? Attract buyers using a low price, or by exposure and marketing? Most sellers who end up confused at the process, and frustrated with a home that failed to sell, never realize that they violated Law # 1 without knowing they even had a choice to make.

> **Alice:** *"Would you tell me, please, which way*
> *I ought to go from here?"*
> **The Cheshire Cat:** *"That depends a good deal on*
> *where you want to get to."*
> **Alice:** *"I don't much care where."*
> **The Cheshire Cat:** *"Then it doesn't much matter*
> *which way you go."*
>
> ~ Lewis Carroll, *Alice in Wonderland*

Anyone can "list" your home. Selling it for top dollar is something totally different.

There are really only two approaches to selling a home. Price or Marketing. The easiest is to price it low enough that a buyer bumps into your home, likes it, and buys it. The most effective, but much harder way, is to actively go and find ALL the buyers who might buy it – not just those that are easy to find.

There is no fixed selling price for your home. The ultimate sales price can vary widely. Your choices determine if you'll be on the high or low end.

Nearly every agent sells homes by price. I'll explain. First they look at past homes that have sold, show them to you, and then convince you to stick your home at the very bottom of the "list" and wait ... and wait ... and wait. Almost no exposure ... just slap it up on the MLS, and use the low price to catch the attention of a buyer.

If the home doesn't sell, they ask you to reduce the price. You agree, and then wait. In another month, you reduce the price again. Eventually, you'll "suck in" some bottom-feeder who'll be happy to "steal" your house. This is a painful process – but it does work, and has for a hundred years, however, it's an expensive way to go about it.

Sellers are constantly misled to believe their home will sell at the same price, no matter what they do. If you don't purposely choose the Exposure route, this is where you end up.

What if you use another approach? Exposure, or what I call the Marketing Approach. You still need to price within a reasonable range of value, but you're going to sell your home by driving traffic to it.

Think of the Price Approach as similar to a man relaxing on the banks of a stream with an outdated fishing pole ... he can still catch a fish if everything works out perfectly. The Marketing Approach is like having sonar, nets and the best equipment possible, working upstream pulling out fish by the net full ... leaving the poor fisherman on the banks, *hoping* to catch a fish that gets past the net.

Is *hope* really a strategy? Not when it comes to selling your largest and most expensive possession.

Whether the market's up or down, there is no fixed price for your home. There's a huge 22% price range that your home could sell for, based on how 168 different variables are managed. Most people in real estate are overwhelmed by this, so they continue to sell homes by price-cutting.

Real estate markets will move up and down over time. Regardless of the market, homes always sell within a price range. In most neighborhoods, values range from 11% below to 11% above. Even if the homes are similar in size and features, there are still a number of variables that impact the final price.

Now 22% is a big swing. For example a "$400,000 home" can sell from $356,000 on the low end to as high as $444,000 if you control all the variables. $88,000 is a lot of money to lose.

The great news is that knowing these Seven Laws and your choices impact almost all the factors it takes to get to the top of the 22% price swing. The most important is how you will expose your home to the most active buyers. Do you want your home sitting passively at the bottom of a list, or actively marketed for top dollar?

If you choose to sell by price-cutting, you can stop reading now. Your fate is set. If you want Top Dollar, then you need a proven strategy. The higher the price you want, the more potential buyers you need.

LAW 2 – EXPOSURE THROUGH MARKETING

Sadly, many people who just sell their home will never know of the thousands they lost because they cut corners and only exposed their home to a limited number of buyers.

No Marketing = No Buyers
Minimal Marketing = Minimal Buyers and No Offers
Ok Marketing = Ok Offers
Maximum Marketing = Maximum Home Sale Price

The goal of marketing is to attract the greatest number of qualified buyers, in the shortest amount of time, and position your home to receive the highest offers. To be on the top end of the 22% price swing, you need to position and expose your home to increase buyer demand. More buyers = more money for you.

All marketing is not the same. Real estate marketing does not equal just putting your home on the Multiple Listing Service. Real estate is a numbers game. That means reaching the most qualified prospects for your home across the top methods.

Marketing is fluid but some of the best methods right now include leveraging relationships with top brokers in town, extreme signage, super-charging your property exposure through cutting edge Internet marketing, interactive voice technology, print, TV and especially radio.

Technology has changed things. The first showing now happens online!

Over 90% of homebuyers use the Internet to search for homes, and 56% said it was their very first step taken during the home-buying process. Yet, according to recent studies in 2014, only 64% of Realtors even have a website.

Most only generate a couple buyer inquiries a YEAR, with the median number being four per year. Only 5% of agents generate over 100 leads per year. WOW! It matters what marketing plan you use to find buyers for your home.

Buyers don't just go to one site. Your home has to dominate the homes you compete against on every website buyers use in their search, or your home becomes invisible and won't sell.

Most agents test their marketing with your home. With a proven plan you are only testing your price, home location and appearance with what buyers have to compare it to. Huge difference.

Everything is marketing! Everyone is marketing! What does the sign say about how serious you are as a seller? Does it say I chose the cheapest agent who works part time at the local deli, or as a cashier at the salon? Did I choose the agent who works for the cheapest broker in town? Most agents are only able to sell several homes a year and might be treating your home sale as a "Hobby."

LAW 3 – FORCE MULTIPLIER

If there was an emergency expense and you had to sell everything you had over the weekend at a garage sale, would you put up one sign? 10? 100? Would you just put one in front of your house, or all over town? The answer is obvious ... you would put them everywhere because you want as many buyers as possible to attend.

All Seven Laws stand independently, but when layered together, they create a synergy that gives you an unfair advantage in your marketplace.

Force Multiplier is mostly a military term to describe the amplification or improvement of something through technology, or using multiple techniques at once to improve results. GPS is a great example instead of using individual soldiers as lookouts. In real estate, you can go door-to-door looking for a buyer ... or use the phone, mail, email, Internet marketing, etc., to help reach out and find people who might be interested in your home.

Many sellers today fall into the trap of leaving their sale up to a single For Sale sign in their front yard, and hoping a hot, pre-qualified buyer will magically drive by and yell, "Honey, stop the car!"

Marketing multiple places and different ways increases the impact. Like synergy, 1+1 can actually = 3. Each technique builds credibility, comfort, familiarity, confidence and a feeling of attraction. Buyers fear making a mistake. You comfort buyers when they are attracted to your home by different marketing media.

LAW 4 – ACCESS: DON'T BLOCK BUYERS

There are buyers who would be open to touring your home, and prepared to buy it, if they only knew about it.

Growing up in a big city on a very busy street wasn't great for playing in the road, but perfect whenever we wanted to put something in the driveway and sell it. Car to sell – no problem. Garage sale to get some pocket change, piece of cake. Why was it so easy? Traffic, traffic and more traffic!

With hardly any planning and no signs, we had a built-in stream of buyers who would stop and buy stuff. Today I happen to live in a gated community back in a cul-de-sac. Great for teaching the kids how to ride a bike … not so great for a garage sale. Exposure is the key to driving the price to the top of the price swing.

The primary job of a REALTOR® is to cause your home to sell by exposing your home to the greatest number of qualified buyers. Only a fraction of a percentage of buyers buy a home in the same neighborhood, but that is where 95% of most misplaced marketing is targeted. Many sellers today get seduced into hiring a "Neighborhood Specialist" to put a sign in front of their home and hope it sells.

Metaphorically, that would be like me opening up my garage behind the gate, and expecting to get as many buyers as the home outside on a busy street with signs leading to it from all directions.

LAW 5 – PRESENTATION AND PRICE PLACEMENT PRODUCE PROFIT

Some garage sales had everything cleaned and displayed like a makeup counter at Macy's. Others had piles of junk, next to other piles of unwanted clutter. If you treat it like you don't want it, what type of message does that send? Top Dollar for your junk? Not a chance.

Simple staging does wonders for a home. How you live in a home is quite different than how you sell one. It's an inconvenience, but losing thousands is very common when sellers don't think it matters. Quick tip: get an outside, unbiased perspective. Often sellers are too close and emotionally tied to the home to be objective. Think of how, open, inviting and uncluttered staged model homes are … that's the target.

Value is determined by what a buyer is willing to pay, based on the comparison of your house to others on the market, in and around your neighborhood.

This is competition at the highest level. Positioning your home against "better value homes" will cost you thousands. Your home has to be positioned to win – not just be one of the crowd. Want your home to sell for Top Dollar? Then change the sellers who you compete against, and the buyers who see you.

How important is choosing the right price to introduce your home to the market? Very important! Even with the most aggressive marketing plan, if your home is overpriced and not near market value, you're going to be frustrated and won't sell for Top Dollar.

LAW 6 – CREATE A PERCEPTION OF SCARCITY

You know this intuitively. First garage sale you pull up to has nobody there. The second one is buzzing and cars are lined up along every curb, and rubber-neckers are creeping by. So many people hunting you're getting bumped around. You see a rare book that completes a set. The guy in the funny hat sees it also, and makes his move. You get it first.

It's in great shape and priced good at $8. Are you going to negotiate with the seller and offer $5? No way! Not when funny hat man is breathing down your neck. You might even quickly hand her a $10 bill so the price doesn't mysteriously go up. Exactly how real estate works.

To get top dollar, you need buyers NOW, not slowly over time. The best time to get Top Dollar is when your home is first introduced to the market. When a seller says "Let's just try it at a higher price … we can always come down later." I know that's a seller who will leave money on the table.

Farmers say, "Pigs get fat, hogs get slaughtered." Don't be a hog. Price within a reasonable range of value, and your wallet will stay fat and happy.

LAW 7 – EXPOSURE WITHOUT CAPTURE AND CONVERSION IS A WASTE

100% of buyers said that their agent's response time was important. . . . not 99%, but all of them. Up to 80% of potential buyers are lost because agents lack response and conversion systems, so they wing it.

Not only should you insist on proven marketing for your home, but confirm the system to convert leads into sales is working 24/7. You could have the greatest marketing plan in the world, but if interested buyers are lost without converting them from interest to offer, your home simply won't sell.

I will always be grateful for my mom realizing she was not building a collection of trinkets – she was building a young man. I hope you never look at a garage sale sign the same again. When you look to sell your home, I hope you make the profitable choice to obey the **Seven Laws for Top Dollar.**

About Curtis

Curtis Johnson runs a highly successful real estate team at Curtis Johnson Realty, having sold over 3,000 residential homes. *The Wall Street Journal* ranked his Team as one of the Top 50 out of 1.2 million REALTORS in America. He is frequently referred to as Arizona's Top Real Estate Marketer (see www.RealEstatesTopMarketer.com) online, in national interviews, and in mainstream media.

He is one of the most connected and sought-after real estate minds in the business. Over the years, Curtis has been a headline speaker and trainer at some of the largest, and most cutting-edge real estate events in America. He has shared the stage with top coaches, motivators, and out-of-the-box strategists, both inside and outside of real estate, giving him a unique perspective to solve problems as a consultant to many real estate top producers across the country.

Top media personalities such as Barbara Corcoran from ABC's hit TV Show Shark Tank, the number two and three 'most-listened-to' radio hosts in America, Sean Hannity and Glenn Beck, have all vetted and endorsed Curtis and his home-selling strategies.

Battling the free falling market in Arizona convinced Curtis he needed a new approach to helping his clients instead of just following the same broken models available. Huge portions of the real estate community left for the safety of calm waters at home … seeing an opportunity, but more importantly a need to bring solutions to struggling homeowners in pain, he went to work to find the best way to attract more buyers to their home, and get them "Top Dollar."

After years of dissecting the real estate transaction and discovering the key elements that affect the sale, Curtis flipped the typical real estate transaction on its head. He systematized the process with his exclusive 89-Step No-Risk Home Sale and 47-Step Home Discovery and Acquisition Method. These two exclusive programs give Curtis and his Team a huge advantage when competing against both average agents and seasoned top producers. Nobody in the market has solutions as comprehensive as Curtis Johnson Realty.

His extensive knowledge of the real estate market make him an in-demand speaker and real estate expert. He constantly analyzes current market conditions and trends to stay one step ahead of others in the field. Curtis holds several advanced professional designations, including GRI, ABR and CRS.

Curtis has been featured nationally on the cover of *REALTOR® Magazine*, prominently in *CNN Money Magazine*, and alongside hosts of HGTV, as well as interviewed locally on virtually every TV station and newspaper. Curtis and his selling system have been featured on the "60 Minutes" equivalent in several countries internationally. For years on radio and TV, Curtis has been the voice of reason trying to make sense of the Arizona housing mess and recovery.

Curtis was raised in California, enjoys sports, competing at almost anything from Monopoly to video games, reading, marketing and spending time with family and friends. He is active in the community and loves serving in his Church. His wife Marilyn and three energetic sons (Daxton, Derek and Treyson) revel in the great weather and lifestyle that living in Arizona affords them.

CHAPTER 8

THE LOST ART OF PRICING A HOME

BY CHRIS JACKSON

The National Association of Expert Advisors tells us the average homeowner could be leaving as much as 18% of their equity on the table, and up to 80% of homes are selling below asking price! You may ask yourself why that is.

I learned early on in my career you will do one thing in life as a real-estate professional, and that is either create a raving fan or cost your client a lot of money! I have seen this too many times early in my career in real estate. What alarms me the most is the homeowner doesn't even know how much they have lost.

I have recently listed a property that was amazing and was on the market for 362 days. Needless to say, the owner was tired of keeping the home in a model-ready state for almost a year. As a real estate professional, we all know what goes through our minds – something was wrong with this home – possibly foundation, wallpaper, yellow and green cabinets, or a major highway in the backyard.

As I pulled up to the property I had to make sure I was at the correct address. I looked down at my notes and called the office to make sure I had the correct file. I was in disbelief this property was on the market for 362 days in the neighborhood where it resided. It not only was a great location, but the school district was voted number one in the state of Texas. The city was voted as being one of the best cities in the country to raise a family.

As I walked up to this home and knocked on the twelve-foot solid oak door, it slowly opened. I was greeted with a half-smile from the homeowner. You could see that she was leery on what I was going to say about her home. After getting the grand tour of the 5000 square foot home, I was looking for what was wrong. I was hoping to find a clue as to why the home didn't sell. I was offered a drink, which I gladly accepted. A good rule of thumb, never deny a gesture of hospitality. This is an invitation to build rapport and trust with your potential client. We then moved to the twelve-seat dining room table so I could get to know the homeowner better. At this point I was in the mindset of truly showing this homeowner I was invested. I needed to find out what her motivation was to sell the home, and why she thought the home didn't sell.

She took a deep breath and started telling me her story. I listened and allowed her to get it all out. She began to get very emotional as she was telling me this was her *dream home*, but it was just too big for her and her mother who was elderly and moving slow. I was told very early on in my real estate career that we don't sell homes for a living. We are in the business of helping people. After spending time with this homeowner, it was crystal clear what my part in all this would be. After our talk came to a close she looked at me with a tear in her eye and asked, "Can you help me?" She stated that she was tired and didn't know if she could take another year of her home being on the market. I stood up and gave her a big old Texas bear hug and told her to start packing. We listed the property, had three offers and I sold the home in fourteen days for list price.

There are situations like this happening all across America in the real estate industry. As a real estate professional, it is my fiduciary responsibility to make sure I represent our clients and know the markets inside and out. When hired to represent a homeowner in the selling of their home they have entrusted me to lead the process, and in most cases, with the largest investment they have. In order to direct this process and to ensure the home is priced correctly and positioned in the market to have the most exposure, there are five laws that if followed, will give you the edge over the competition in the marketplace.

I. THE FIRST LAW IS BUILDING RAPPORT

In order to really understand the Law of Rapport you must first understand the definition of rapport: "A close and harmonious relationship in which the people or groups concerned understand each other's feeling or ideas and communicate well." This is where asking the hard questions becomes crucial. Some may ask what rapport has to do with pricing a home. I say to them it has everything to do with pricing a home. If the homeowner doesn't trust you and feel they have a connection with you, you will never be able to establish the worth of your expertise when it comes to pricing their home. Some of the hard questions may be: why they are selling, what are their financial goals, past experiences and what is plan B if the home doesn't sell. In the above-mentioned account, I was able to build rapport with the homeowner simply by being a good listener and allowing her to tell me her story.

II. THE SECOND LAW IS SETTING EXPECTATIONS

This law puts all the cards on the table of what to expect throughout the process of pricing their home and what goes into it. One thing to realize is that the only way this law will be effective is if you build great rapport and trust with the homeowner. They must view you as an expert – much like a doctor is to his or her patient. They may not like what you say, but they respect your opinion and counsel. Always remember that the homeowner, in most cases, will have an emotional tie to their home – and believe it is worth more than the data and what the market will show. It is vital that you present a solid plan of action, with expectations knowing that things will not always go as planned. Here are some great points that will help you not only win the listing, but also keep your homeowner from becoming that fire-breathing dragon! First: set check in times once a week for the first thirty days. I call this my touch points. You can create touch points by a simple phone call, email, just checking in card, automated market updates, or if you're in the area drop by and say hello. These touches will continue to build rapport and trust, so when there is a perceived problem they will at least allow you to state your case. The homeowners will always love you until the showings slow down and the home doesn't sell quickly enough to meet their perceived expectations, despite the expectations you set. One thing my mentors Jay Kinder and Michael Reese always told me was if you say you're going to do something, you better do it. If there is turbulence during the process, and there always will be, refer back to the expectation all parties agreed upon in the beginning. Here is an example of how that may sound:

"Mr. and Mrs. Smith, when we first spoke we all came to an agreement of how we were going to manage the selling of your home, would you agree?"

"Yes."

"Great! Let me ask you a question. What has changed in your situation that we need to address?"

III. THE THIRD LAW IS
THE DEATH OF THE CMA

Death is a very strong word, and that is why we use it. Death is final. It has meaning to it and gets the attention it deserves. Real Estate is changing in so many ways. That fact that 90 % of homes are viewed online first should tell us something. The data in a CMA is still good to pull and is very useful, but to give value to a home based on a CMA alone is like driving a car looking in the rear view mirror. Here is a list of items that a CMA does not take into account: condition of the property, underpriced, dated interior, highly motivated seller, divorce, improper marketing, curb appeal, foreclosure, and short sales. These are all items that if allowed, will lower the value of the home substantially, and have a negative impact on the equity the home will bear. The fact is simple: anybody can sell at the bottom of the market, however, it takes expert knowledge to sell a home at the top of the market. Another very valuable tool I use frequently is to have several appraisers in my network and use them as an advisory tool to help dial in on how the market is performing. They, in turn, use my expertise on what I am seeing in the market place to help with their side of the business. It is vital that you understand how an appraiser thinks and how they look at things when it comes to pricing a home.

IV. THE FOURTH LAW IS SUPPLY VS. DEMAND

There are so many factors in this law you must weigh against when pricing a home in today's market. When inventory is low (a sellers' market), you will in most cases be able to adjust accordingly to capture the top of the market. When the number of homes on the market exceeds the number of buyers (a buyers' market), you will have to be on your "A" game and sharpen your negotiation skills. Here are some items you need to be aware of when evaluating supply vs. demand: numbers of homes on the market, number of homes entering the market, absorption rate, number of home selling in specific price ranges. This is just to name a few. You must be a master of collecting data and evaluating that data in order to position the home to capture the highest possible offer.

V. THE FIFTH LAW IS POSITIONING

This is where "the rubber meets the road," where the game is won, and where all your hard work pays off. This is the reason you are considered an expert in the field. And, as you start the journey of creating the life you strive for, remember when you change your thinking from how much money you can make to how many people you can help get what they want, your income potential will be monumental in comparison. Throughout this process you will have positioned yourself as an expert and what you say will matter. Building rapport, trust, giving expert advice will not only help you and your client, it will help you with negotiating offers. So let's get started on setting the stage of preeminence.

How do we set ourselves apart from the pack. First, you must have the home professionally staged. What I mean by staging is to hire a professional certified stager, this is not for you the agent to do. This practice alone can increase the sale price of a home by 6-10%. It can also decrease days-on-market up to 50% as well as increase perceived value and attract multiple offers.

Professional pre-inspection also will set you apart from the pack. We all know what it feels like waiting for that inspection report to come with the laundry list of items. This is a major "deal-killer" in our industry today. It is better to know what's under the hood and price the home accordingly, than to get an offer and have to discount the sales price by thousands of dollars when it should have been repaired for half the cost.

Professional photos are a must. Agents taking their own is not the thing to do in today's market. Remember over 90% of homes are viewed on-line first. If the homes photos do not look appealing or enhance the homes features, you're going to end up at the bottom of the list of homes to view. Even if the home is undervalued, you run the risk of collecting unnecessary days-on-market, which in turn will hurt the positioning of the property as well as the perception of value.

At the end of the day you must put your heart and soul into what you do. Helping clients get the home they have always wanted is rewarding in itself. By following these five simple laws you will not only change the lives of your clients, but impact the lives around you.

All in all, *be first class with your service and you will obtain first class results!*

In conclusion:

See you at the TOP!

About Chris

After graduating from Southeastern Oklahoma State University in Durant, Oklahoma, in 1996 with a double major in Advertising and Public Relations, Chris Jackson soon married his college sweetheart Hollie, and in 2000, their first son Christian was born, and 18 months later came along their youngest son, Colby. Chris was a very dedicated career executive which put him in a position of authority with several Fortune 500 companies. Chris found himself at the negotiation table often and gained the reputation known as a closer. It would not be a normal year without having to negotiate several multi-million dollar contracts.

With more than twenty years of experience specializing in contract negotiations, sales training and marketing, Chris' life soon headed in a different direction. Chris attracted the attention of the Founders of The National Association of Expert Advisors: Jay Kinder and Michael Reese. Chris was brought on board to help lead the upcoming brokerage of Kinder Reese Real Estate Advisors based in Frisco, Texas. Needless to say, his real estate career was on the fast track being mentored and coached by two of the industry's leading brokers. Chris is part of the Kinder Reese executive team, and is on pace to sell 75 homes this year.

CHAPTER 9

CREATING WEALTH THROUGH REAL ESTATE

BY KATE (PREETI) BRAGANTI, COMMERCIAL AND RESIDENTIAL BROKER

Back in 2001, my life experienced a substantial shift. In a short amount of time, I went from being a married, stay-at-home mother of two, to a divorced mother of two. **I needed to find a career, and QUICK!** I'd moved from my native country of India in 1993 (then known as Preeti Singh), and did have a college degree in Fine Arts and English Hons. They were of little value when it came to earning an income. *I was faced with no knowledge about the outside world.* Also, I'd never been put through any test to see *if I could make it on my own.* I had no choice other than to find a way to MAKE IT! I had to take the western world by the horns and **boldly step** where I'd never gone before. Thankfully, my parents helped with my children, so I could seek out a career that would bring me joy and happiness. *No one was more surprised or delighted than me when I realized that real estate was my passion.*

Real estate is an immense field, and there are many agents out there with different specialties or focuses; some have none at all. I knew that I had to find something to specialize in and begin pursuing it with everything I had. It was necessary to CREATE DISTINCTION between myself and the many others working in real estate. The one area that really stood out to me and captured my fascination was using real estate as an income-earning investment tool. *I wanted to find clients properties that performed!* By doing this, I could help others build wealth to make them independent of their 9-5 jobs (if they wished to be), while offering them proven knowledge and experience in both residential and commercial investment real estate. **The results have been amazing – giving me a wonderful career, and incredible repeat clients and referrals.** It's exciting for me to share some of the fundamentals that help ensure real estate investments are successful. *Anyone who commits their time, resources, and remains focused can build a sound portfolio that will generate wealth for them.*

YOUR TEAM IS EVERYTHING

If you have ever thought about entering into the real estate investment arena, I want to share <u>one important thing</u> that you should not do immediately. That is: NEVER be your own agent.

> There are a portion of investors that believe that if they get their real estate license they will be able to save 2%-3% on their investment costs. This may be true upfront, but *you could lose substantial amounts of money in the future.*

On average, it takes about 90 hours of education to get your real estate license. That doesn't give you experience, it gives you a license. A license doesn't equate to being a professional. **Work with a trusted and proven professional!**

In order to understand the legitimate, essential expertise that an experienced professional in investment real estate can offer, you need to realize what they are providing you. These are things that *I've been providing clients on a consistent basis for over fourteen years.* THEY WORK!

WHAT EXPERTS OFFER

Not every investment property is what it appears to be on the surface. **What looks like a good deal "now" may be a very bad deal "later."** How do you know? You may not, but an investor-savvy Realtor does. They understand that you must evaluate a variety of things, each one is an important part of the equation.

- <u>Knowledge of market</u>: Your investment team must know what people are looking for, how to connect with good properties, **and have made favorable negotiations an art form**. *There is a much greater market for investment properties than what exists on the MLS.* There are also:
  - Distressed properties, which can turn out to be a gem
  - Foreclosures
  - Rentals
  - Auctions

- <u>Mentorship</u>: The best Realtors are not selfish with what they know. They want to educate their clients, teach them what's important about investment properties, and *create a partnership*. As a real estate buyer, you should expect to receive:
  - Insights that save you time and money
  - A roadmap to help you create the success you are striving for

- <u>Understand the numbers that show what is a sound investment</u>: Buying a property is an investment, whether it's first time home buying or for an income-generating opportunity. **You always want to be in a position to profit**, and your expert Realtor can help you achieve that. *You do this by becoming an equity buyer*, which <u>keeps the emotional aspect out</u> and allows you to objectively evaluate a property, keeping in mind maintenance, warranties, inspections, lifestyles, the right lender, and the right mortgage to help you build equity faster. Plus, expert advisors help you find the right property at the right price and work with you to avoid hidden landmines such as liens, easements, and encumbrances. They focus on lifestyle and neighborhood profiles that are suitable for you and your investment.

Experts will leverage the most result-oriented negotiation strategies favoring you to buy your home with absolute best possible price, terms, and conditions. In real estate, there is a right way and a wrong way to do most things. If you want to succeed and want to make money then you need to learn to do everything the right way. **It's a numbers game and it's absolutely essential for your success and making top dollars**. You need to know cash flow, rate of return, property value, and financing guidelines—and that's just for starters!

Whether you're a buyer, seller, or a mortgage lender, knowing a property's real worth is important. This process varies. Single family homes focus on what a house is worth, whereas investments are all about "net income." Investors don't decide to buy properties, they buy the income streams of the properties with anticipated economic benefits. Experts know how to do this efficiently and effectively; *it's more than an educated guess*!

MUST KNOW CALCULATIONS FOR INVESTMENTS!

1. Gross Scheduled Income less Vacancy and Credit Loss = Gross Operating Income
2. Gross Operating Income less Operating Expenses = Net Operating Income

There are two known elements to a property evaluation: Net Operating Income (NOI) and cap rate, which is the rate of that return.

NOI represents a return on the purchase price of the property. It also expresses an objective measure of a property's income stream, while the required cap rate is the investor's subjective estimate of how well his or her capital must perform. Below are two figures to visually show the meaning of NOI, relaying what it includes and what it doesn't include, as well as what significance it has to your property's worth.

Figure 1.1

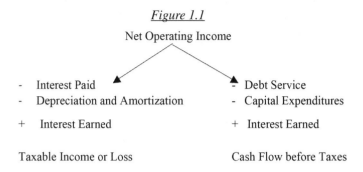

Net Operating Income

- Interest Paid	- Debt Service
- Depreciation and Amortization	- Capital Expenditures
+ Interest Earned	+ Interest Earned
Taxable Income or Loss	Cash Flow before Taxes

Once you know the property's NOI, you branch off in one direction to determine taxable income and in another to figure its cash flow.

Figure 1.2

Taxable Income and Cash Flow

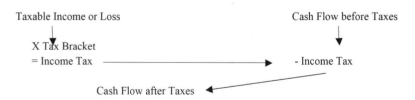

Taxable Income or Loss   Cash Flow before Taxes

X Tax Bracket
= Income Tax ————————————→   - Income Tax

Cash Flow after Taxes ◄————

THREE AREAS OF FOCUS FOR REAL ESTATE INVESTING

You've thought about investing. Now find out what it takes so you know if it's the right choice for you. You don't want to become a "burnt out" investor because you didn't understand the entire process. **Be informed**. Understand what can go wrong and possible outcomes!

1. Build a sound portfolio.

The way to build a sound portfolio is to *have an idea of the parameters that work for you*, as well as what doesn't. This can be achieved through *building a blueprint to set your criteria in place* and then compare any properties you may be interested in against it. If all the pieces do not fit, be comfortable realizing that the property may not be as "ideal" as you are hoping it is.

2. Invest your time and remain focused.

Here's a common example of someone who enters into real estate that isn't focused and hasn't invested the proper amount of time:

The bubble comes and you enter the rat race, thinking that you will make money like the others that you've heard about— those lucky people! You make an assumption that it will all come together. You believe that real estate is a "get rich quick" gamble, one that most people win. This mentality will almost always lead to disastrous results. Investors who start investing with this preconceived notion will do maybe one or two deals in a year and then they're exhausted. That house they wanted to flip doesn't sell in 90 days. It sits on the market substantially longer, leaving an ill-equipped owner who may not be able to deal with the costs and stress that ensues. It's a bad experience. ***It's also an experience that can be avoided!***

Building real estate wealth takes time. It doesn't happen in the blink of an eye and *it isn't a "get rich quick" opportunity*. Sure, maybe you will get lucky once, but that luck will not continue on. Real estate investing takes time to develop and grow, like a mutual fund, and it isn't designed to be instantaneous profit like you might get in the stock market, for example.

3. Have a vision for the long run.

Take some time to think about bigger companies—those with big visions—and <u>understand how they approach their business</u>. Do these companies only think about the next year or two when they plan? No! They look ten years out and **focus on creating a structure that is built to last**. This is how you should approach your real estate portfolio. Eventually, it will be on auto run, but it won't start out that way. PLAN ON SPENDING 4 to 5 hours every day on this business in the beginning.

How do I know all these things? This is a fair question and I encourage people to ask me when I start working with them. I entered into real estate in 2002 and have created a full-time career out of it ever since. *I've survived the ups and downs.* Good times and bad times have happened, but **I have managed to help many clients achieve their dreams**. I have remained focused on the important fundamentals that make for sound investing. As you look for a proven Realtor to become a part of your expert real estate wealth team, you should **ask them questions about how they've survived the ups and downs**. It says a great deal about their business practice and their character. I want you to have success and that's why I am letting you know this!

HELPING SELLERS MAXIMIZE
THEIR TRANSACTIONS

So far, I've talked about how expert Realtors such as myself are very impactful for buyers, but we are also essential to a seller's success. There are four aspects of selling a property that a smart seller will embrace. These aspects are all achieved with the guiding hand of an experienced Realtor that understands the business and their needs.

Expertise: Since real estate professionals are the key factor and your best advisor, you want to choose the right one. Knowledge is important. Passion and expertise are essential. Don't settle for a Realtor who doesn't possess these qualities. We know that there is only one thing a seller wants—RESULTS! Real Estate Expert Advisors will position your property in the market and won't base this on a CMA (Comparative Market Analysis) alone. They also evaluate the outside threats and consider all the aspects of supply and demand that impact the pricing and sale of a property.

Differentiation: Creating differentiation means **more money for sellers**, more savings for buyers, plus *faster and better service to the consumer*. Peace of mind during a transaction is an intangible that can only be achieved with the help of an expert Realtor.

Exposure: Attracting buyers who will pay the most money means you must have a plan to give exposure to the property that reaches the most highly qualified buyers. Experts know how to do this effectively!

Negotiation: There is an art to negotiation and it's a powerful tool that allows you to position yourself smartly. With the right mindset, and the proper expert Realtor, a winning situation can be created, that combined with the other factors of cooperation and acquisition, can bring 18% or more for your property.

REFERRALS AND TESTIMONIES
CREATE TRUE VALIDITY

There is no greater way for us vested Realtors to receive confirmation *that what we are doing does matter* and **makes peoples' lives better**. Receiving positive feedback this way allows Realtors such as myself to really show our prospective clients that we do deliver results. *Testimonials and referrals confirm our actions, not just support our words*. And the thing that is really amazing about referrals is that you can look at a few as a nice compliment and motivator; however, when someone continues receiving them and they emphasize what someone is striving to achieve, it's evidence that you've come across a special formula that will work! I wanted to share a recent referral

I received that really ties together the message of what I always hope to achieve for my clients:

I would, without reservation, strongly recommend Kate and her team. Kate is responsive, knowledgeable, courteous and highly competent. She knows the Santa Clarita market and her business thoroughly, and is state-of-the-art in every respect. She cares about her clients and her service doesn't stop when an offer is accepted—her follow through on all the complex aspects of completing the transactions and meeting all the current regulatory requirements was exemplary.

It doesn't stop here, she has a great team of vendors and free Utility Concierge Service where she makes moving smooth as silk. I feel great that I am well in time and I can enjoy Christmas in my New Home with my Family, and I am convinced that we found a perfect house and a great deal for our dollar value, and I attribute that to her expertise.

I even listed my current house for lease with her and within 15 days of listing the property she closed it, and I already have a tenant with full asking price. I can't imagine buying or selling a home without her team.

~Kabir B.

MY MESSAGE TO YOU

Everything I do for my clients is because I am vested in their experience. It means so much to me and I get so much joy from it. I love real estate dearly, and I live and breathe it daily. Without these steps and assurances, my business would not be what it is today, and more importantly, I wouldn't have been able to help hundreds of people achieve their real estate goals over the years. ***It's more than client satisfaction, it's showing clients that I am willing to invest my time into their success!***

About Kate

Kate (Preeti) Braganti found her professional home when she entered into real estate in 2002. She was instantly drawn to the potential she had to help clients achieve their real estate goals through her taking the initiative to become an expert. The field of expertise that Kate committed to was investment real estate. She hasn't looked back since. Today she is a commercial and residential broker/owner of Aarnaa Real Estate, Aarnaa Finance Group and Aarnaa Investments, Inc.

It is Kate's firm belief that in today's real estate market you must be specialized. As a member of National Association of Expert Advisors (NAEA) and through the direct mentorship of Jay Abraham for marketing, she has been able to create a 7 Star Service plan that keeps her in the spotlight as a producer in the San Fernando Valley and Santa Clarita Valley, a market she knows extremely well. Kate is grateful to her team, who helps to make this all possible. Without them, success would be a much more challenging journey, if not impossible. In addition to NAEA, Kate is a member of the following organizations:

- Strategic Marketing Master (Jay Abraham)
- National Association of Realtors
- California Association of Realtors
- Southland Association of Realtors
- SCV Chamber of Commerce
- Khalsa Care Foundation

Kate believes that life and career are all about passion, and she breathes it for real estate each and every day. This is all due to her clients. Kate says, "All the accomplishments wouldn't mean much without creating happy clients along the way." At present, 60% of Kate's business comes from positive word-of-mouth referrals from past clients.

In her personal time, Kate is a passionate reader, fitness enthusiast, and an avid traveler who has seen half of the world—the second half still to come. She is continuously inspired by other cultures and the people she meets while visiting them. Furthermore, having these experiences with her son Ishneet and daughter Pragati by her side, creates very special memories that they cherish and look forward to every year. For stress relief and to remain at her personal best, Kate also leads a meditation group that gives its members positive focus, clarity, and joy.

One other aspect of Kate's life that is profoundly meaningful is her involvement with charity. She is a strong advocate for underprivileged children and families, and reaches out to homeless shelters to help, all while inspiring others to do the same! Her meditation group has set a goal to help others by collecting nonperishable items when they meet to help those in need. She personally has also created a goal to raise $5,000 increments of funds as often as possible, so they can move families from shelters into apartments. Her goal is to do this at least twice a year. If you'd like to learn more about Kate (Preeti) Braganti's services, email her at: kate@aarnaa.us or call: 661-435-7100 or 661-444-3700.

CHAPTER 10

FROM LISTED TO SOLD: HOW TO GET TOP DOLLAR FOR YOUR HOME

BY STEVE ZAHND, REAL ESTATE BROKER

Many people view the equation of selling a home as a rather easy one. You take a few logical steps and then wait for the offers to come in. This would be fantastic, and a small fraction of sellers will experience success this way, but what about the rest of the sellers out there? They don't want to rely on luck. They are better served relying on working with Expert Agents who understand the full compass of what it takes to sell a home with fewer hassles and bigger returns.

There are three major factors that empower buyers to want to buy a property with confidence. Each one of them is an essential part of an effective strategy to sell a home for maximum dollar and minimum negotiations. Make sure you are seeking out the Expert Advisor (also known as Realtor or Listing Agent) that understands these concepts. *It will make your home selling process smoother and more successful.*

MAJOR FACTOR #1:
EXPERT ADVICE AND MARKETING IS EVERYTHING

This may be hard to realize, but there is a wrong way to market your home, and choosing the inexperienced or under-experienced agent, or a *For Sale By Owner* shop to attempt this, is a costly mistake. The process involves more than taking a few pictures on a camera or phone to upload to the Internet, writing a nice "homey" description, maybe doing a print ad, and placing a sign in the yard. This method leads to frustrations for sellers. They become frustrated with their agent, their home, and the process as a whole. No one wants that! We all want results. Sellers need solid guidance and direction on how to get results, and this is more difficult to find than many imagine it would be. Not all people who call themselves Realtors understand the full scope of the process.

Marketing your home requires expert advice and a sound strategy. Below are four important points to comprehend and draw from when marketing your home.

1. 80% of the real estate agent population, including *For Sale By Owner* communities, are frustrated because they do not get the complete picture. To them, marketing is spending the most money you can—nothing more. Any marketing agency can tell you that there's much more to the science of marketing than that. It's no wonder that most people believe real estate agents are overpaid. They become complacent or lazy or just do not have the knowledge necessary to be effective. For example: as I am writing this chapter, I have received an email from an agent offering a 40% referral fee if I have a client for their market. This only demonstrates that they believe they are overpaid and are not willing to invest much of their time or energy into creating optimal results. I would never send my clients to this agent because they are clearly not investing in tools to optimize systems which will lead to greater bottom-line dollars.

2. The right tools help bring the right results. At my brokerage we are obsessed with this because it has consistently proven itself to deliver optimal results—solid offers. What do we do? It's simple. **We negotiate before you even start negotiating!** I know what you are thinking, *this guy is crazy. That doesn't make sense.* But if you really think about it, it does, and *the question you should be asking isn't how, but why.* There are a few things that everyone should ask of an agent that they are considering for a home listing.

You should ask:

- *What type of pictures and video do you take?* High quality pictures and videos are important and the iPhone photos posted to the Internet are not going to work in a seller's favor. Furthermore, lack of a full video walkthrough of the property is a negative, because it does not show the property's full potential.

- *Do you research the perfect buyer profile when preparing marketing?* No one can market to the masses using a singular approach. Targeted marketing that reaches out to a legitimate potential buyer will always be better.

- *What do you recommend for staging my home?* This is important because there are certain ways to show your home more favorably than others. Presentation is everything, and buyers connect with houses that they envision themselves living in and creating their own memories in—the memories that make it a home.

- *Are there any investments I should make in my property before listing it?* There are times when an upfront financial investment is necessary to get the most appealing offers on a home. If you want top dollar, your property has to be in the condition that reflects that. Inspections before listing a property are a great way to know what you are working with and will take away the buyer's ability to counter negotiate.

- *Why should a buyer pay top dollar for my home?* This is a blunt question and an agent who doesn't go through the proper marketing steps will struggle to answer it. Be a smart and informed seller because it will help you pick the agent that wants the same results you do.

3. Put yourself in the buyer's perspective when it comes to selling your home. If you want the highest consideration for your home, you want to make sure that people see the ultimate value in your home above another. That helps people feel confident in their decision to put their highest bid on the table to win your property. That is what we want buyers to feel like—a huge winner! Think about it. If you are going to the grocery store and you see a beautiful red, ripe tomato—picture perfect tomato A—and another tomato that is almost perfect but getting a little soft, tomato B, which one which you pick up? The one that looks perfect, right? Despite just a small, seemingly unnoticeable visual difference, you are just completely more confident that tomato A is the right choice, that tomato A is the one that is going to deliver your desired result and meet your expectations. You are confident about it, and guess what? I bet you wouldn't even think about asking the cashier for a discount. Why would you? It's perfect. You want buyers to think of your house like they think of tomato A.

4. Never underestimate buyer confidence. It matters greatly when it comes to getting top dollar for a home and the market you choose to sell your house in will determine your results. Knowing you want top dollar, are you going to position yourself in mediocrity? There's plenty of it out there, but that is not what you want. Always remember:

- Choosing to go *For Sale By Owner* automatically puts you in a position of reduced demand. On average in my market, *For Sale By Owner's* literally only have 5% market share. Plus, they are not overseen by a regulatory body which is obsessed with consumer protection and also has a constant push to make

Realtors further regulated, further educated, and further developed to ensure customer security and satisfaction. This makes buyers more leery of "do it myself" sellers and guess what, many agents are leery of them, too, because they do not know all the regulations. You could be isolating that ideal buyer by thinking you should do it yourself and not call in the help of an Expert Agent.

- Be mindful that buyer confidence is not just related to security and peace of mind, it is also associated with how the product that buyer is purchasing fulfills their expectations. Educated buyers research before they buy. They dig deep and have a plethora of information available to them via the Internet and other sources. Once that buyer finds something they are interested in, they will compare it to their list of expectations. Then they determine whether or not they have full confidence to move forward on a product. The more confidence the buyer has that a product will fulfill their expectations, the less price will be a concern.

- Is the property you own maximized to fulfill your potentials buyers expectation list? Or, will it fall short in one or two areas? You get that buyer who wants your property and is putting the offer in. They request an inspection (and they will!) Maybe that inspection reveals an ugly truth that was hidden from the naked eye. What happens then? Confidence is hit hard. Questions and doubt literally rush into the mind of the buyer and suddenly you have lost all of your control over the negotiation. That full price offer you have on the table is in major jeopardy of dropping in price or even worse, being pulled all together.

If you want to inspire buyers to put offers in on your home you need to market to the best prospective buyers and get a feel for how they react and what they do. Put yourself in their shoes—especially if you are looking for a new home as you sell yours—

would you react any differently? Unfavorable marketing leads to a lack of buyer confidence, which leads to a stagnant property that is not moving. The back and forth negotiations that lead to surprises and delayed closings do not have to be a part of a transaction. They are a part of the old, traditional linear path. Unfortunately…a majority of sellers are still resistant to working with an Expert Advisor over their Uncle Joe or Cousin Suzy— the part time agents who want to earn a few dollars here and there helping their families and friends. What do they do? They just click over here, hammer a sign over there, snap a picture, and bam—the house is sold. Wrong! This myth has haunted the real estate industry for too long and it has resulted in sellers losing tens of thousands of dollars. It's the exact opposite of top dollar.

MAJOR FACTOR #2:
PREPARE YOUR HOME TO DRAW THE HIGHEST, BEST OFFERS BEFORE IT GOES TO MARKET

This strategy is the most underutilized one in the real estate market, in my opinion. If there is nothing else that I can get a seller to take away from this chapter, it is that you must prepare your home if you want to attract high quality, full price offers. Did you know…

The strategy of preemptive negotiation is the ultimate boost to tangible and perceived buyer confidence.

Preemptive negotiating is exactly what you need to embrace if you want to get top dollar for your home. This strategy is a series of tactical processes that has been proven to rocket buyer confidence and comes right out of the second law of home selling—the law of differentiation.

Most agents will employ one or two of the strategies that are going to be listed out below. It is rare to find agents who are not Expert Advisors that will perform all of the listed tasks for you, plus have trusted connections that will carry out the duties with the highest level of professionalism and execution.

1. **Staging:** Staging a home is not just about placing furniture or putting fresh paint on the wall, it is having a trained expert that understands what buyers want to feel and think when they walk through the front door of a home. Setting up your home for maximum buyer appeal can add 6% - 10% to your perceived value. That sounds good, doesn't it?

2. **Quality of Life Upgrade Analysis:** Depending on budget, it is important for homeowners to invest into key areas of their home before it hits the market. During this process, a true real estate expert will identify improvements that can be made which will have a high impact on the home's value.

3. **Pre-inspection:** Once a house is in order, a pre-inspection is the next critical move. It is a preemptive negotiation strategy. It's better for a home seller to know about any potential deal killers ahead of time and try to circumvent them by fixing the problem. If there are no problems when the buyer has their inspection there is not going to be any price renegotiating. Sellers need to strive to remain in control of negotiations. This tactic has proven to yield 2% – 4% higher perceived value in the home because potential buyers know that all concerns have been dealt with and the house has a clean bill of health.

4. **Warranty:** Getting a home warranty is a smart move. After a home is inspected and any defects corrected, the house is eligible for a home warranty. This is a big boost to buyer confidence because the buyer knows that the home has been inspected, corrected, and warranted. The buyer will have one year of top to bottom coverage and this brings peace of mind. Buyers want to spend their money on making their new house a home, not dealing with unexpected expenses.

5. **Professional photography and videography:** The last piece that ties it all together is to get expert photos and a professional full video walkthrough. With the majority of

buyers starting online, it is imperative to get those buyers confident enough to get off their computers, get in their car, and see your home in the flesh. No one buys a home without seeing it and no one wants to go see a home that doesn't look good online—unless they want to negotiate you down to a very low price.

MAJOR FACTOR #3:
HIRE AN EXPERT ADVISOR

The condition of the house is important and everything in this chapter has expressed why. However, that is not all it takes to go from listing to sale. You also need to hire an Expert Advisor if you want to ensure that buyer confidence stays intact throughout the process. The Expert Advisor will:

- Navigate you through the process
- Ensure that you do not sound desperate to sell—which is a huge red flag
- Show all the reasons why your house is one that any buyer can be confident in

Most of us demand and expect experienced professionals to deal with the things that are most important to us in our lives. We want a doctor to help us medically. We demand our cars be repaired by mechanics who know what they are doing. When it comes to selling a home, why would a person sell themselves short by having someone who does not understand the nuances and best strategies to sell a home? Expert Advisors love what they do and it shows in how they walk sellers through the process of selling their home with informative, insightful, and helpful information to get their sellers that coveted great offer.

About Steve

With a fresh approach to real estate success, Steve Zahnd is committed to finding ways for consumers to experience a positive real estate experience. Early on in his career, Steve realized that the real estate industry was in need of professionals who gave reliable advice to their clients, not just told them what they wanted to hear. Why risk such boldness? He wanted results, not just contracts to list a property or represent a consumer.

Back in 2011, Steve really focused on what he could do to ensure he had the real estate success he desired, not only for himself, but also his growing family. He went to work with a well-known real estate franchise, surrounding himself with the best of the best. He wanted to absorb knowledge and was submersed in learning how to give buyers and sellers the ultimate real estate experience. He quickly realized success, receiving recognition that is rare for someone so new in the industry to achieve, including: Masters Silver Award (2012), and Centurion Award (2013).

As business grew, Steve's abilities to lead others to better real estate success grew, too. A single man's effort turned into a team of seven agents who all carried the same fresh approach to real estate success. Steve has doubled his business year-over-year since earning Masters Silver in 2011. He then took the next step to create a real estate environment that stands apart and on results, and opened up Zahnd Team Real Estate Advisors, Inc. in late 2014. Prior to this change, the Zahnd Team would have earned the Double Centurion Award if they did not leave their real estate franchise to open their own brokerage, doubling their business once again.

Today, Steve focuses on adding only two agents per year to create a strong team of experts that do not conflict with the company's culture, along with highly-skilled administration staff, which is essential to a successful real estate business. It's a very interactive process, one in which the entire team supports each other, realizing that a strong team makes everyone more successful. This is appealing to consumers who are seeking out the most professional real estate agents to handle their transactions. It is also a big draw for Realtors who wish to grow a real, sustainable business.

Steve makes his business and home base in Guelph, Ontario, Canada. When he is not at work there is nothing he enjoys more than spending quality time with his family, experiencing all the amazing things that Canada has to offer culturally and in nature. Steve is also a coach for his son's baseball team, loving to use his leadership skills for helping to inspire young people to be better at the things they love to do. During the slower real estate seasons, Steve often takes advantage of the opportunity to escape the cold weather and create special family memories in warmer locations; something that many people can appreciate who live in a blustery winter environment.

CHAPTER 11

HOPE WON'T GET YOU TOP DOLLAR!

BY DWAYNE GROSS

*Our goals can only be reached through a vehicle of a plan,
in which we must fervently believe, and upon which we must
vigorously act. There is no other route to success.*

~ Pablo Picasso

In 2009, shortly after President Obama had taken office, CBS News posted an open letter written to him by Dr. Benjamin Ola Akande. Dr. Akande is an economist and the Dean of the Business School at Webster University in St. Louis. In his letter he sought to advise Obama about how to get our country back on track. His title for the letter: "Hope is not a strategy." This idea was not new to me but Dr. Akande said it so eloquently that it became a quote I think of often in relationship to my own work.

One summer during college, my mom grew frustrated with my summer agenda. It was pretty typical for a nineteen year old guy – I was enjoying time with friends and relaxing. Mom suggested that I make my summer more productive; and as a real estate agent herself, she had just the plan for me. She told me to study for and earn my real estate license. And with that act of frustrated parenting she led me into my career in real estate. That was twenty four years ago and I've never been sorry about taking her advice.

A rule in my family is that if you wanted to be part of the family real estate business, you had to go and work for another company first. It was important to my mother that we had first-hand, real world experience . . . experience outside the umbrella of our family-run business.

Early in my career, when I was just learning the ropes, I went out on a listing appointment with an older agent named Joe. He met with the couple that owned the property, listened to what their goals were for selling, and secured the listing. After that meeting, we were walking the property and placing our sign in the front yard. As we left I asked him, "So, now what do we do?" He laughed and said, "Now we just sit back and we hope someone sells it for us." He had no marketing strategy other than to rely on hope to sell that home.

This event took place in the early 1990's and the housing market was in terrible shape. One might think this would lead an agent to work twice as hard to sell a house, but not Joe. Because that was my first experience and I knew almost nothing, I thought, "If selling real estate is this easy, I've died and gone to heaven. Just put a sign in the yard and wait." I don't think we ever sold that house and that's when I learned, for the first time, that hope is not a strategy – and it's especially not a marketing strategy.

My eyes were opened again when I finally got my first listing. I was in control. But within the first meeting I realized that the seller's expectations were higher than I could have imagined based on my experience learning from some of our more seasoned agents. Expectations on behalf of our clients have only grown. Today the seller pays a significant amount of money and they expect us to have a certain level of professionalism and expertise. They want us to help manage their transaction, but they also expect us to get them *top dollar* and they want the process to be easy.

When I realized what my clients' expectations were I turned things around quickly. I sought to meet all of their needs and to advise them, as well as I knew how, with regard to the best ways to show and market their homes. My hard work and dedication to meeting the needs of my clients paid off. Soon, I was the top producing agent in the company.

Sometimes I think about what I would do differently if I could go back to that property I visited with Joe – The "Hope" Property. I would have invested in landscaping and giving the property better curb appeal. I'd have done a home inspection even before we listed it. And of course, I'd have used whatever tools I had at my disposal to market it!

I believe that the best agents are going to be willing to advise their clients about how to get top dollar for their property. To do that often means making an investment in the sale and marketing of that home. An average agent is going to put a sign in your yard and show the house to the people who call; they will put your home on the Multiple Listing Service so that other agents will see it, and then they will wait. A great agent, one of the top agents, is going to go far above and beyond that.

The best agents know that you only get one chance at a first impression. Sometimes buyers drive past a property that is beautiful inside because it lacks curb appeal on the outside. Seller's may be reluctant to put more money into their home for landscaping and painting the front door, but those two things, done well, can stop a buyer in their tracks. When it comes to first impressions you want to be at the top of your game!

The outside of your home is important, but this requirement extends to the inside of your home, too. Let's say your fabulous landscaping gets them in the front door but they enter to find a mess or a stained carpet. Or maybe they notice that the fifth step on their way to the basement is loose. We don't want or need to give buyers reasons to keep looking or not to buy our home when there are simple remedies for minor problems like these. When it comes to first impressions, you want to be at the top of your game every time someone comes in to see your home . . .

you want it to look perfect! You want to make it look like you cared about and loved your home. This shows the buyer that you took care of it. Knowing that the home was loved and cared for has a positive psychological impact on the buyer and makes them more likely to buy it.

But what if your buyer isn't driving by, what if they're shopping for their next house on the Internet? When people are shopping on the Internet they can see the inside *and* the outside of your home. And all they have to do is click to move on to the next available home in your neighborhood and price range.

Some agents believe that there are certain times of year when it's best to sell. You may hear people say that selling your home in the spring or summer are ideal because that's when schools are on summer break or because that's when the flowers bloom. I don't believe that. I believe that if the agent has positioned the property properly in the existing marketplace then it will sell whether it's January or Christmas Eve or Thanksgiving or Easter. Top-selling agents are selling homes twelve months out of the year on a consistent, predictable basis.

An agent should also help you make your home show at its very best online. They should begin by offering you expert staging advice – that may be advice directly from the agent or a referral to a professional stager. It may seem silly, especially when your friends and family regularly compliment your great taste and your collection of shiny hubcaps, but staging will help your home appeal to everyone – not just the people who know you.

Photography and video are possibly the most important part of your online listings. The best agents will offer you both photographs and video – sometimes the video consists of all of the photos sewn together into a slide show. All photographs should be professional – inside and out - and the photographer should be trained to do real estate photography. The right photographer will know just how to photograph your home so that the photos show all the best features and make buyers want to visit it. Recently a few companies even started using unmanned aircrafts to get the very best images of the exterior of the homes they're listing.

While we're on the subject of your online listings, you should know that the best agents will go above and beyond to maximize your property's online exposure. With 95% of all buyers today using the Internet to look for a new property, it isn't enough to just market your home on the Multiple Listing Service. That service is available to agents but not to the general public. At our agency we market all of our listings on Google, Yahoo, Bing, Trulia, and Zillow. We also put our listings on our own websites as well as some of the unbranded websites, for example, "Homes for Sale in ABC County." Top agents and agencies will also offer mobile applications that people can use to access listings.

In addition to online marketing efforts, an agent should actively market your listing to their database of homebuyers with an eye toward contacting anyone in their system looking for a home like the one that you are selling. Finally, all listings should be marketed heavily to the top 20% of the brokers in the market place. Those are the individuals who are selling the most and they will be able to help you find a buyer.

Maximizing exposure comes at a cost to the agent. A willingness to invest money in your clients is what separates the average agent from a high-producing agent. The agent who invests in well-planned, high-quality marketing and advertising, makes the most money. Bottom line. The average realtor spends about $125 on marketing each month. Many companies have budgets for marketing that far exceed that number. Why aren't more agents using it?

The very best agents will help sellers make their home show well and capitalize on all available marketing outlets in addition to offering two other services: a pre-inspection and a home warranty. Agents should schedule a home inspection before listing the house so they know where problems might be. Then they can address them early on, often at a lower cost. This is one way that clients save money in the long run and are more prepared for the sales process.

Home warranties cover mechanical systems during the listing period, and typically for one year after the purchase of the home. This simple service, typically paid for by the agent, gives the new owners peace of mind because the sellers are providing them with a free year of service and repair to any mechanicals in the house. There's a sense of security there that will attract buyers.

Even after learning what the best agents do to help you get top dollar for your home, there are still sellers who want to try their hand at selling their home on their own. They may have done some research and feel quite confident that, by using the local FSBO (For Sale By Owner) website, they'll have all the exposure they need.

What agents know is that statistically, the people who sell their homes on their own earn 15-20% less than if they'd worked with a real estate agent. And, no matter how many books they've read, the average person lacks the real-world experience an agent has. That experience goes a long way!

Recently, a man who wanted to sell his house reached out to me to help him. I went to visit him and he had a nice little ranch-style house. After a walk-through and gathering some additional information, I told him he could list it at $309,000. He was pleasantly surprised that he could list his home for that much.

About a week later, I went back to visit with him again. I assumed he would be ready to list the house very soon. When I arrived he said, "You're not going to believe this but a neighbor approached me to ask if I was selling the property. He knew my mom had passed away. And…I sold it."

I was surprised that he'd made this decision and I asked what price he'd gotten for the sale of his mother's home. He told me his neighbor paid him $260,000. He explained that he sold it for less because he knows the neighbor well and selling to him just seemed easier.

By not listing with a broker, he sold his mother's house for significantly less than it was worth. He wanted to make the sale easy and, in this case, I could sympathize. But generally speaking, when sellers list on their own they lack one of the skills that agents hone over years: negotiation.

It's extremely difficult to negotiate face-to-face. In the story above, it was especially tough because it was with the neighbor he'd known for twenty years and he was selling his mom's house just after she passed away. He was in a very weak position through no fault of his own. He would have found such value in a third party joining the equation to insulate the buyer and seller and achieve top dollar. You're not going to achieve top dollar negotiating with the neighbor who knows you well, because you won't feel comfortable asking for more.

Even the top agent in the country will tell you that you're only as good as your team. If you are a single agent, working on your own, you're the only one working to sell a property. If you take a vacation, your homeowners are effectively taking a vacation from selling their home. That's not good for business.

Great real estate teams will have individuals who do a variety of different jobs that, when combined, help sellers reach their goal of selling their house more quickly, more easily, and for *top dollar*. Typically they will include buyer specialists, seller specialists, transaction coordinators, listing coordinators, processors and marketing staff. This makes the process of selling property feel seamless and stress-free for your clients.

As the team leader, it's the agent's responsibility to make sure that everything is running smoothly. Every aspect of the transaction – whether it's the listing component, the contract or the closing – is critical and needs to be managed thoroughly and carefully.

Perhaps putting up a sign and hoping that a property sold worked years ago. Perhaps it didn't. Regardless, I can tell you that selling real estate in today's market requires an agent who is dedicated to doing whatever it takes to satisfy the needs of sellers and earn their trust. Hope alone won't make that happen, but hard-work, dedication, and making the most of the tools you have will.

About Dwayne

Dwayne Gross is a Top Producing Real Estate Professional in the Bucks County Pennsylvania area. Bucks County, located 70 miles South of New York City and 35 miles north of Philadelphia, provides an ideal location for commuters. Bucks County has beckon many to call it home with its rich historical references, 200 year old stone farmhouses that remain an intrinsic part of the landscape as well as its breathtaking scenic vistas that have made an impression on many an artist's canvas. Bucks County has been home to Dwayne for over 40 years. His care and consideration for his hometown has lead him to a successful career helping to relocate his neighbors and greeting new ones to the neighborhood.

Dwayne Gross has consistently been recognized by a Worldwide Real Estate franchise for achieving the highest level of sales by volume in his marketplace within the franchise. Gross has also been awarded for his commitment to excellence and quality service an achievement reached by less than 1% the 100,000 real estate agents in the franchise. A self-described Real Estate enthusiast Gross has delved into just about every aspect of the real estate business.

Gross, a Top Producing Real Estate Agent, is also one of the Founding Partners in a Mortgage Company and Title Insurance Company, Real Estate Developer, Investor owner and property manager of several apartment buildings and Managing Partner of a Building Group that concentrates on building New Homes throughout Bucks County. When he is not involved in the day to day real estate business Gross can be found spending time with his wife Carole and daughters Abigail and Emma. A lover of the outdoors Gross is an avid golfer, skier and salt water fishing throughout Central America.

CHAPTER 12

RECEIVING, NEGOTIATING AND PRESENTING AN OFFER

BY STEVEN NIEVES

The primary goal of any listing agent should never be to sell a house. Anyone can sell a house. A weak agent or a strong agent can sell a house. A homeowner can sell a house. In all honesty, depending on the market, a basic sign in the front yard can sell a house. So, what, you may wonder, is the primary goal of a listing agent? Representing the sellers.

All listing agents have a legal and ethical responsibility to perform at the highest level and represent their clients with integrity and great care. Always be mindful of the fact that you are dealing with your client's most valuable asset and pay close attention to even the most intricate of details. Even the smallest error can result in losses of thousands of dollars.

Building on your experiences and learning how to avoid past mistakes in the future will be key to successfully negotiating top dollar for your sellers and avoiding contracts that fall apart through the process. The simplest way to do this is to understand the steps.

STEP 1: RECEIVING THE OFFER

How you handle offers as they come will ultimately depend on what type of market you happen to be working and how long the home has been out there. Oftentimes, the key to a successful and smooth transaction is identifying the strongest offers and recommending those for consideration first. *A common mistake many Listing Agents make is to focus solely on the most profitable offers and pay less attention to the strength of the offer.* Not understanding the kind of offers that will be submitted leads to a single-sided view of the deal and can end up costing you and your client a lot of time and money.

You might not consistently have the same number of solid or credible offers all the time, but ultimately, the process remains the same. Whether you are dealing with a Buyer's Market or a Seller's Market, you need to understand the *5 Basic Offer Types* you will be receiving on behalf of your clients. They are:

Cash or Conventional Offers with 20% Down

These offers are usually your strongest buyers and have fewer obstacles to face, such as appraisers, lender-required repairs or third party-required qualifications, etc. Remember, the less time it takes to get the deal done, the more money your client will save in the long run.

Conventional Offers with Less Than 20% Down

Still traditionally strong offers, a conventional buyer has a stronger credit history and usually less chances of the contract falling through. Conventional financing qualifiers must have a credit score of at least 680.

FHA Offers

Buyers using an FHA loan are looking to purchase the property as their primary residence and will mostly be First-Time Home Buyers. They usually have a higher debt-to-income ratio than those going through conventional financing, and are coming with a minimum down payment of 3.5%.

VA Offers

An individual looking to purchase a home with a VA Loan will be much more restricted on the homes and allowable discrepancies due to the strict nature of the program. Properties in less than "great" condition will often result in a dead deal due to disapproval from the VA or a laundry list of repairs required to be completed before the purchase can move forward and most at the seller's expense. In addition to having to cover the closing costs and pay for various inspections and tests (i.e., Termite and Well Water). An offer of this type, while still valid, often means less profit for your client.

Down Payment Assistance Offers

By far, this type of offer comes saddled with more requirements than any other type of financing. With higher debt-to-income rations, limited funds, and a history of longer transaction times, avoiding such offers is usually the safest bet for your clients if there are any others on the table.

STEP 2: INTERVIEWING THE AGENT

Let's be honest, there are a lot of different types of agents out there. Personality conflicts can be a nightmare when it comes to negotiating a real estate transaction. The best way to avoid finding yourself in an endless loop of painful phone calls for a month or more is to have a quick conversation with the Buyers' Agent submitting the offer.

An immediate call to confirm receipt of their client's offer demonstrates your own professionalism and sets the tone for the type of prompt communication you expect to receive throughout the deal. If it takes days for you to respond to their initial communication, they will start to believe this is the pace of your business and react accordingly. Remember, time is money for you and your clients and starting a potential transaction this way is bound to cause you headaches down the road.

A successful agent interview is comprised of these four basic questions:

How long have you been working with your client?

As simple and elementary as it seems, you can learn a lot from how the agent answers this question. The concern is not really about the amount of time they have been working for the buyer, but how much rapport they have developed throughout their time. Of course, usually trust between a client and their agent comes over time, but don't discount the agent's ability to make a strong impression after just a few meetings. Listen to the pauses, the "Um's", "Well's" and even the confidence (or lack thereof) in the agent's response. Hesitation is a strong indicator of a lack of familiarity, which, in turn, will often mean the agent has less influence on their client's decision.

Is this your client's best offer?

Sure, the agent is really not supposed to disclose this information but you would be surprised at what the agent will tell you if you just ask. If the agent understands how desperate the buyers are to own this particular property, they will often reveal much more than usual in an effort to have their offer accepted. Whether you receive a response indicating they are willing to go up as high as the original asking price or one that maintains an air of mystery, either will still give you more information. This is exactly what you want in a negotiation and will help you navigate the process with more confidence, should your client choose to accept the offer.

Is this the first offer you have presented for your client?

A purchase of this nature can cause people all kinds of hesitation. Feeling good enough to submit an offer doesn't always translate to a smooth transaction. If the buyer has already submitted multiple offers, then you have to identify the cause that resulted in those offers being rejected or withdrawn and therefore resulting in this most recent attempt to purchase a home. It could be they just didn't come in strong enough on their last few attempts and couldn't get an offer accepted. Or, they might have canceled previous contracts due to inspections. Either way, obtaining this information will give you an idea if the offer will *stick* once it's accepted. If you sense the buyers are overly critical or merely settling, be aware of the issues that may arise as a result.

Have you worked with your client's lender before?

If an agent has little to no relationship with a lender or financial institution, you can be sure they will have zero control over their end of the process. Although the steps for completing a home loan are virtually the same, each lender typically has their own processes. If the agent has connected their client with his/her preferred lender or they have had experience with the lender in the past, then you can often count on their knowledge to assist in the deal being completed quickly and efficiently. If not, you could easily be stuck in a sea of uncertainty and frustration. In the end, agent control of the process is huge.

STEP 3: INTERVIEWING THE LENDER

Gathering information from the lender is a key step in the process of preparing offers to present to your sellers. Remember, the more thorough you are with these interviews, the better you will be able to guide your sellers to the best offer. As soon as you have obtained the answers you need from the Buyer's Agent, you can begin to tailor your questions for the lender accordingly. A buyer's agent should have a good amount of information regarding their current loan status, but to effectively present an offer to your client, you need to make sure you have a deeper understanding of the seller's financial situation.

Here are five items you need to clarify with the lender when you initiate contact via email or a quick phone call:

Proof of Income

Make sure the buyer has the funds available for purchase. This usually includes an overview of their most recent pay stubs or bank statements. If the proof of income does not support the income stated on the application, this is a red flag and you will want to be careful proceeding.

Employer Verification

A lot of things can happen between a buyer's initial pre-approval with a lender and the time they finally place an acceptable offer on a house. If the buyer has had a change in employment, this can create issues with finalizing the loan or delays that will end up causing issues with the entire transaction.

CAVRS Report (Credit Alert Verification Reporting System)

In the case of government loans (VA, FHA, etc.), you will want to make sure the buyer has not had a foreclosure in the last three years that will prevent them from receiving a loan approval. Government guidelines are much stricter than conventional loans, and ensuring there are no past issues will help your deal close much quicker.

IRS Transcripts

It's always tempting to write off larger portions of your annual income to get that bigger return from the IRS. It's not just the self-employed either. Even W-2 employees find what they can to write off when tax season rolls around. Unfortunately, if a buyer has done this, it can mess with their debt-to-income ratio. So, it always best to verify the lender has checked on this before moving forward.

Credit Report

Most lenders are going to be more protective of this type of information but if you can start with a generic question, you'll be amazed at what you can discover. It's usually best to find out when the buyer's credit was pulled last. Credit can change dramatically in just 60 days, so it is good to be aware of these types of future complications well before you present the offer to your client. Most importantly, though, is to ask for the buyer's credit score. Even though the lender is not supposed to disclose this information, there is still about a 50% chance they will let you know. If you can't get it, don't be discouraged, you have still obtained plenty of information to help you dutifully assess the offer.

STEP 4: PRESENTING THE OFFER

Once you have completed the interviews and gathered all the pertinent information, you are ready to submit the best offers to your client. If you are fortunate enough to have multiple offers, it is best to counter at the full asking price. In a single offer scenario, you have fewer options but should still feel comfortable countering at 98.5% of the asking price (depending on the price point).

The goal is to continue to keep the process moving so constant communication and regularly met deadlines are key to a speedy closing. In most cases, it is recommended to include an inspection period of no longer than 5 to7 days.

After your seller accepts the most favorable offer, it would be in their best interest to accept a back-up offer. This continues to give your client options and a promising purchaser if things don't work out with the first offer.

Finally, have your seller sign a *net sheet*. Your goal in representing your client, the seller, is to also make sure they have a clear understanding of the commission, tax and title fees, and what that will mean for them in terms of their net profit once everything is finalized.

Ultimately, a successful real estate transaction will depend on your ability to invest the time up front, focus on the details and extract as much information as you can from the Buyer's Agent and Lender. When you begin to master this process, you will see a much higher rate of conversion on accepted offers and end up saving yourself and your client a tremendous amount of time and money.

About Steven

Steven Nieves began his real estate adventure in 1999 becoming a licensed agent in the state of New York and receiving the Rookie Of The Year Award his first year. He has shown consistent growth and productivity and managed to maintain an increase in sales even as he transitioned from the New York to the Texas real estate market.

To date, Steven has sold more than 1400 homes and has maintained an average of 85 homes sold per year. In the last five years, his sales volume has totaled more than $140 million and he has sold an average of 135 homes per year. This is nearly a 160% growth, which he accomplished in a turbulent market. He has won multiple real estate awards and become an expert in negotiations, short sales and relocation services.

Steven attributes his success in real estate among today's fiercely competitive marketplace to his unique *Team Partnership* concept. Unlike a traditional real estate agency, he has assembled a diverse staff of real estate experts and support specialists who deliver more personalized services to their clients while working at a higher level of proficiency.

At the core of Steven's basic principles for success is his ultimate desire to provide excellent customer service to all of their clients and rely heavily on repeat and referral business to grow his team. He encourages steady communication between his clients and all the members of his team, and has developed a solid foundation of fiercely loyal clients in the process.

Steven resides in Dallas, Texas with his wife and three daughters, and has focused the majority of his business growth in the Dallas/Ft. Worth Metroplex.

CHAPTER 13

TOP VALUE FOR YOUR HOME

BY RICHARD REID

Selling your home for top dollar in the shortest amount of time is a great sound bite. In my experience, most people are really after generating the greatest *value*. Realizing maximum value in real estate - like much of life - is part science, part art and part luck.

Since all real estate is owned by someone, each deal is unique. This necessitates that the definition of value is special. The minimum components driving the nature of the deal are the specific situation of the selling party and the nature of the property itself. All property occupies a geographic position that is different from all others - even if the floor plans, designs, etc. are all identical.

There are three components we need to understand to begin to shape the ideal transaction for someone looking to sell real estate:

1. What is the ideal sale date for the Seller?

2. What is the target sale price for the Seller?

3. What is the Seller's motivation for the sale?

THE SALE DATE

The book implies the best sale date is the earliest sale date. There are some generic truths to this. Deals that close faster tend to have fewer issues. The sooner the sale date, the quicker the realization of the profit – which affects the time value of money. There is a shorter period a Seller might have to live through showings, or wonder if the potential Buyers liked the home. To be sure, if the Seller is looking to get out of the home in the shortest period of time - or if they have already moved out, the fastest closing date is of greatest value.

Let's test this theory, though. The generic answer is the shortest time, but what if the home the Seller is moving to, is being built, and the construction won't be completed for 60 days? In this scenario, they might be forced to move out of one house, pay a moving company for storage, find temporary housing, and be cramped in an unfamiliar space with children for a period of time. What is the incremental value you would have to receive to make this type of experience worth it to you?

Many people have both a home to sell and a home to purchase. If they cannot purchase without selling, the variables at play become significant - in particular if the market they are moving to is a hotter market than the neighborhood they are moving from.

Life is complicated. Since most real estate transactions are concerning someone's primary residence, that makes real estate deals, negotiation, and strategy somewhat complicated. It's important to understand that something as simple as a date has a ripple effect on how a transaction will play out. The real and emotional costs involved in the potential impacts can and should be considered as a part of the value equation in a real estate transaction.

As you consider the timing of your sale, make sure you share important dates and impacts with your agent. There are ways to affect timing early in a listing or deal that may have very little negotiation cost. Often when you are deep in the negotiation, the impact of such changes can come at a much greater cost.

THE TARGET PRICE

Price is the most obvious component a Seller is likely to think about or consider as part of a real estate transaction. We need to break price into two segments - what the seller thinks, and what the market is telling us.

Sellers pay most attention to the top dollar - the offer price, but there are many factors that affect the real price - the net price a Seller may receive. Let's look at the following examples:

1. Is the Buyer requesting any closing cost contributions from the Seller? If so, these will need to be deducted from the offer price.

2. Is the property being purchased "as-is" or is it subject to repairs? If repairs are in play, what is the cost of these - both in terms of dollars and the time and effort it takes to manage the repairs.

3. We've discussed dates as a practical exercise, but it affects this formula as well. Are there any mortgage payments or costs associated with maintaining the home between the offer date and the closing date? These will need to be considered.

4. What impact, if any, does the closing date have on where the Seller is headed next? If there are incremental costs or special costs to accommodate a less than ideal situation, those should be reviewed as a part of the offer.

5. Is the Buyer requesting a home warranty or any other special contributions?

6. What other items are in the contract with an actual monetary value?

7. What items in the contract have real dollar implications to the Seller?

8. Are there items that have an emotional or effort value that can be considered as a monetary factor?

9. Can the home appraise?

When you are considering the sale of your home, it is important to understand the many factors that define your situation, and to share those with your agent. If a good agent knows this information, they can better serve you in the positioning and negotiation of a deal that will truly create the best value - not just the highest top line number.

We will attack the market perception of value after we consider the balance of the Seller's driving factors.

THE MOTIVATION

Motivation is one of the most important and least considered factors in a real estate transaction. It drives behavior at the core, and hence, the negotiation process. Without understanding the "why", it's almost impossible to arrive at the best outcome.

In many cases, the "why" in real estate is a life-altering event. Real Estate often changes hands with the birth of a new family member, a marriage, a divorce, children moving off to college, people in new relationships moving in together, etc. Some of these come with real deadlines, others have softer timelines. Each of these factors is important in a real estate deal.

Before listing your home, consider what's driving you. Is it simply moving to a home that better suits your current needs, or is there a life-altering event at play? Are there fixed dates that are significant in the process? What's your financial cushion to deal with any delays or drama that happens during a transition? How do you process money and the type of stress that accompanies your home being in flux?

The answer to the why and how you process uncertainty will provide greater insight into how a home needs to be listed, marketed, and how a deal needs to be negotiated. It's important to find an agent who is willing to take the time to learn these factors, and who is well suited to bring balance to the transaction.

THE EMOTIONAL FACTOR

Emotion wasn't in my original three points for this segment, but I'm offering it as a bonus - because it almost always surprises people. The topic at hand is real estate, but we are usually talking about your home. Whether you've lived in a home for 6 months or 60 years, a certain amount of bonding has occurred. People react differently when the property being negotiated is this intensely personal.

I've worked with numerous clients who are attorneys, accountants, CFO's . . . individuals who deal with legal contracts, high dollar transactions, and critical decisions for a living. Each of them loses perspective at some point during the purchase or sale of their home. While there are an infinite number of contributions a good real estate agent can bring to a transaction, it's the emotional factor that keeps agents in the business. Without a buffer between Buyer and Seller, more deals would fall apart than stay together.

In some cases, core reactions in a transaction go back to motivation. Other times it simply is emotion - memories that have been built in a home or the reality of the life-changing event. Approach the purchase or sale of real estate with the understanding that it will get emotional. When it does, allow yourself the space to process those emotions your way, and you are likely to have a much more positive experience.

You don't have to pour your soul out to your agent, but you need to provide them enough insight that they can help you, give you the space you need, and smooth things out in any deal in progress.

MARKET VALUE

At any given point in time if there is a ready, willing and able Buyer who will pay a price and meet terms required by a ready, willing and able Seller - neither of whom are under duress or distress, the price at which the home sells is Market Value.

If only it were that simple, things would be great, but there are other parties involved in the determination of value - namely banks / mortgage institutions, appraisers, real estate agents, and all of those people in the neighboring transactions in recent history. So let's explore this a bit further.

When most agents begin to work on a price for a listing, they perform what is typically called a CMA (Comparative Market Analysis or Comparable Market Analysis). It can also be called a BPO (Broker Price Opinion). All of these are performed by real estate agents or brokers. They differ from actual appraisals because of the form utilized and because only an appraiser's assessment of value can be used for any of the primary lenders in the United States.

In almost every case, these analyses will look only at historical data for the determination of value. Looking backwards - so long as things are moving up - is the most conservative way to approach value, and that makes financial institutions comfortable.

Let's go with the assumption that it's a normal market for the moment and look at some of the components of a good CMA Appraisal:

1. Recent sales - ideally within 90 days.

2. Within the same neighborhood - as defined by your area. In some cases this is within 1 block, while in others it could be within 2 miles. Context is king.

3. Ideally the homes are within the same natural and man made boundaries.

4. Same zip code.

5. Same school district (are there any changes happening in the school district?)

6. Similar styles of homes - this goes to conformity.

7. Homes in the same community or communities with similar amenities like being gated, having swimming and tennis amenities, or if you are in a city, the walkability of a home or neighborhood.

8. Similar crime statistics.

9. Similar commute times to likely employers.

10. Similar square footage of both the home and the lot.

11. Similar bedroom / bathroom counts and relationships.

12. How long did each of the homes take to sell and where were they priced relative to the competition?

The closer in feature, function, and value the properties are to each other and to the home being evaluated, the more likely accurate the report. As adjustments come into play - which is inevitable - the decisions can be highly subjective.

Now that we have the components of a decent market analysis, it's important to understand that this may not have nearly the defining effect one might hope for. Remember, these are historical indicators. Before we do anything else, we need to understand the position of the home we are considering relative to what is on the market right now. Is there more competition or less than when each of those homes sold? What is the market like right now? Are there plenty of buyers? How does your home appeal to the market relative to the other offerings?

Markets are almost always trending up or down. A good price will reflect those changes - whether they are above or below the historical data. Time of year may affect your market, though this is typically a smaller effect than most people imagine (outside of resort markets).

At this point we have a historical understanding of value, an understanding of value relative to the properties on the market today, and some clarity on the market trend. With these factors, we need to circle back and review the Seller's motivation, ideal move date, and their perception of price. If they are in line, things can seem pretty straightforward. If there are discrepancies, there are a number of ways to resolve the gaps, but simply wishing the numbers were different is not one of them.

As people live in a home, they fail to see things age. If they are not actively looking at homes, they tend to miss trend changes and the significance of having a home feel current. When there is a discrepancy between a Seller's target price and the Market Value, this can be one of the simplest things to address. Often updating fixtures, painting, some minor refinishing and deep cleaning can have a significant impact on the market perception of a home. Sometimes it's necessary to go further with more extensive upgrades, though the risk should be considered carefully. It's often less risky for a Seller to adjust their price down than to invest significant dollars where they may not make the return they hoped.

If you are struggling with where your home's value is relative to the price you hoped for, a simple way to gain clarity is to visit other homes in the immediate area currently for sale. Pretend you are a buyer who wants to live in this area, and then create a pro / con sheet for the homes on the market and think about what you would personally be willing to offer them for their home relative to their list prices. Then think about your home. Would your home be your first choice? If not, where would it fall in the list? How much different would the price of your home have to be vs. the competition to make it your number one choice? Objectively? The emotion has to come out of the mix here as much as possible.

Remember as you work through all of these exercises that this is one of the largest financial undertakings you have likely made to this point in your life. It is foolish to do so without sound advice from a trusted advisor. You need a solid advocate in your corner. This may or may not be your best friend who has a real estate license, or the person you play tennis or bridge with. It needs to be someone who works in real estate full time. Someone who has their pulse on the market, current trends and issues affecting the market, and that has a solid track record.

Whether you are in a market that I serve (currently Atlanta and Decatur, GA) or somewhere else, I provide educational material to buyers, sellers, and agents in an effort to raise the level of service in the industry.

About Richard

Richard Reid realizes his clients' real estate hopes and dreams through his unique approach to the market. His entrepreneurial upbringing makes him uniquely qualified for this task. Richard grew up in a family where owning your own business was assumed, and he enjoyed seeing his parents create several thriving businesses. Through his career, Richard has excelled in the worlds of retail banking, automotive sales and finance, software development, and real estate. Real estate is his stated profession and passion because it leverages all of the previous careers.

Richard's personal real estate practice is centered in the Atlanta and Decatur markets. Here he works with buyers and sellers to deliver an entirely new level of service in the real estate industry. Richard is able to leverage his understanding of finance, 20 years of living in the market, and 10 years of selling Atlanta real estate together with custom real estate software tools and proven real estate processes that allow his clients to save countless hours per transaction. He has developed a team of professionals to provide consistent service at every point in a real estate deal.

Richard developed training and educational materials to offer a curriculum and a path to agents looking to dramatically improve their real estate business. "The Ultimate Buyer's [Agent] Blueprint" features eight CD's, a manual and workbook laying out best practices for building a successful buyer's agent business.

Richard was featured as an expert in the real estate documentary "Selling America" for which he won an EXPY in Media & Communications from the National Association of Experts, Writers, and Speakers. He has also been featured on ABC, CBS, NBC, and Fox affiliates across the country as a real estate expert – most recently with Bob Guiney on the TV show "Success Today." In 2014, Richard was recognized as one of the Top 500 Marketers in Real Estate by the National Association of Expert Advisors where he has also been recognized for business growth. Richard is also one of "America's Premier Experts" for his commitment to publishing expert content for the benefit of consumers and journalists.

Richard, a graduate of the University of the South – Sewanee, has a strong liberal arts background, a passion for learning, and a drive to educate and empower others to improve their lives. This passion is lived out daily helping real estate clients, building his team, and educating those aspiring to be better agents to serve the communities in which we live.

You can connect with Richard at:
rreid@directlinkrealty.com
www.RichardReid.com
www.DirectLinkRealty.com

CHAPTER 14

HOW TO PROPERLY POSITION YOUR HOME FOR TOP DOLLAR

BY SHAWN CULHANE

Selling real estate may seem simple to the average homeowner. Clean up your house, list it, show it to prospective buyers, agree on a price and let the bank take care of financing, right? Well if you want to get top dollar for your home and sell it in a timely fashion, there are many things to consider and you'll need help from specialists.

Recently our agency sold a home for $273,300. The home was sold to a Realtor® and a few months later the agent who had purchased the home put it back on the market. Something had changed in her life and she decided not to move in. When she sold the house, just five months after buying it, she was only able to sell it for $257,500. She had a loss of 6-percent in that short period of time, but the home and market hadn't changed, so what made the difference?

This didn't happen in 2008 when the housing bubble burst, this happened within the last twelve months. The truth was that she didn't have an effective marketing plan to sell the house and she didn't have a team of specialists in place to help her net the highest amount possible from her sale. Her photos were of low quality. The home was empty and stale rather than staged. It took her twenty days to sell the home while we'd sold it in four. Even this agent could have benefited from hiring an agent. That is, she should have hired one of the top agents in the area. Top agents have proven systems for selling homes that net the homeowner 6-7% more than they would net using a typical, average agent. Past sales performance is always the best indicator for future performance when it comes to real estate sales, so check an agent's sales statistics.

WHY SHOULD YOU HAVE AN AGENT?

When you've decided that you want to sell your house there are a couple of ways to go about it. You can list it yourself as a FSBO (For Sale By Owner) with the help of a few websites, like Craigslist, that allow you to list property for sale. Or, you can look for a professional Realtor® in your area - but not just any Realtor®. If you're going to invite someone to help you sell your home, you want to find someone that is truly an expert and has a proven track record.

When choosing whether to hire an agent to sell your property or to sell it "by owner," it helps to think of the sale of your property as an auction. If five people showed up to an auction for your property, don't you think the sales price will end up being quite a bit lower than if you had 100 people in attendance? When you choose not to hire an agent, it is similar to choosing to only market to 5% of the potential buyers as opposed to 100%. Effective marketing plans that top agents use will expose your property to all potential buyers, not just a few looking for a deal or for owner financing.

According to Dave Ramsey, there is a study on For Sale By Owner homes, which found that the median sales price of a typical home sold "by owner" was $184,000. A 7-percent marketing fee would be about $13,000 on that sales price. The median price of a home sold by an agent fetched $230,000. That's a $46,000 difference. Homes that sell "by owner" are proven to sell for much less, for a few reasons. So much less that one might wonder, if one chooses sell their home without a Realtor® to avoid paying additional commissions and fees, are they really saving money? Is it possible that they're actually losing money?

There are stats that show oftentimes For Sale By Owners leave a lot of money on the table, much more than a commission would equal. From a different perspective, even if a seller is able to net the same as they would, had they hired an agent, that seller just traded a whole lot of their time and money in exchange for absolutely nothing.

Most all experts in the real estate field agree that it is important to have an agent representing you when you're selling your home. The best agents may sell a few homes or more each week, their knowledge and experience will pay off for you the seller.

Realtors® often consider how they will differentiate themselves from their competition. Sellers know that it isn't just about having your home listed on the right websites or hiring someone who claims they already have an anxious buyer. It is important to work with an agent who uses a proven marketing plan and has a verifiable reputation that you can trust, preferably one who also has a team of specialists to help you get the most you can from the sale of your home.

WHAT TO LOOK FOR IN AN AGENT

All agents claim to have a marketing plan, but not all marketing plans were created equally. Most agents use the "Three P Marketing Plan." They Put a sign in the ground, they Put the property in the MLS (Multiple Listing Service), and finally, they Pray that it sells.

Only a very small percentage of agents have an extensive marketing plan and can count on it to help them sell a high number of homes for top dollar. When you are looking for an agent, perhaps the first thing to look at is the agent's business model. You should hire an agent that comes with an entire marketing team made up of professionals who can help you reach your goals, as opposed to a single agent who attempts to wear all the hats necessary to a successful sale.

According to the 2013 Profile of Home Buyers that the National Association of Realtors® compiles, 94-percent of all potential buyers use the Internet to search for their next home. It is imperative that any agency you work with have a strong web presence with featured profiles to highlight their listings. Look for an agent whose brokerage pays the extra fees for the top websites (e.g., realtor.com, which is generally considered to be the most accurate widely-visited site) to place their listings prominently where buyers search. Featuring your property in such a manner is one way to assure that it gets maximum exposure as opposed to getting lost with hundreds of other listings.

Most agents have to manage each part of the listing and sales process alone. Without a whole sales team this is very difficult and it stands to reason that because the sale of your home requires expertise in a variety of areas, no single person can be very effective in every area. Whether or not the average agent will admit it, the fact is that agents who use a team approach are more successful than those who operate alone. Agents are more successful when they have a whole marketing team to support them.

When interviewing agents to sell your property, an important question to ask is how many sales they've had in the past year. Most top agents sell more homes in a week than many people will sell in a lifetime. To become a top selling agent, one must know how to predict potential issues before they happen and come up with a solution. They are the ones that have the experience of keeping a deal together and closing successfully.

Ideally, your agent will be an open book. They'll be able to show you their performance statistics – how many homes they've sold, their average days on market, their average sales price, their average list price to sales price ratio and so on. When you interview an agent to represent you, they should be able to provide you with a wealth of information about their business. In fact, here are fifteen questions you should consider asking before working with an agent:

1. How many homes did you sell last year?
2. What was the dollar volume of homes sold last year?
3. How many homes have you sold this year?
4. What is the dollar value of the homes sold this year?
5. What is your average "days on market?"
6. How many of the homes this year have been sold by representing and marketing a seller's home?
7. How many $ are spent on marketing your listings per month?
8. What is your current listing inventory?
9. What is your average List Price/Sales Price ratio?
10. How many homes are "For Sale" in our market?
11. How many homes sold in our market last month?
12. If selected to list our home, do you have a specific, effective, proven marketing plan for selling our home? If so, please present it now.
13. What specialists make up your team members?
14. Can you provide a list of at least ten references?
15. Can you provide reliable data relating to the current market value of our home?

If your agent refuses to answer the questions or just doesn't know the answer, then they're probably not a top agent. Why would you trust that person with what is potentially your largest asset? The very best agents are happy to share their statistics as they welcome a comparison to the other agents you interview.

THE TEAM APPROACH TO SELLING YOUR HOME

As mentioned earlier, to represent a seller most effectively, it takes a team of specialists. There are several key members of that team. The team leader is the one who orchestrates and manages the structure of the team members ensuring that your needs are met and your home is sold for top dollar.

Offices should have a <u>Pre-listing Coordinator</u>. This person works to prepare your property for listing by scheduling a stager and professional photographer, providing advertising copy to the seller for approval before syndicating that listing to all the applicable major websites. In addition, he or she gathers the seller's disclosure, survey, and other necessary paperwork so that the agent has all the right information on hand when they find an interested buyer.

Another invaluable member of a real estate team is the <u>listing specialist</u>. They will preview your home, and will help determine the overall marketing strategy and at what price to list at. You should have a designated listing specialist as this person will be your main point of contact and typically handles the negotiations between you the seller and the buyer's agent. Good listing specialists may negotiate and sell more than 100 homes each year while previewing 500-1000 homes each year. They specialize in contracts, pricing, marketing and negotiations.

For example, in the state of Texas, there are roughly twenty-two "outs" for buyers in the typical real estate purchase contract. This means there are twenty-two potential ways for a buyer to get out of a contract. When you have a specialist that is aware of this, he or she can address them from the beginning so you aren't surprised later in the sales process. Price should not be the only consideration when it comes to the terms of the contract.

It is usually a good idea to have a property pre-inspected by a third party, licensed inspector regulated by your state. Studies have shown that when you are selling a home that's pre-inspected with corrective action taken for the deficiencies, it helps the buyers feel more confident in their decision and may command a premium. It's much like purchasing a certified pre-owned vehicle and the peace of mind that comes with that.

The marketing team should include a <u>talented interior designer and/or stager</u> who is available for consultations with you about your house specifically. It's not enough for an agent to direct you to a book or a website, they need to have a qualified specialist who can give you real and relevant advice about the décor in your home so that it shows well in person as well as for photographs. Sellers can earn 3 to 4-percent more simply by having their home staged and presented properly.

Once you've met with someone to help you stage your home for the sale, you'll want beautiful photos to provide for the websites where your home is showcased. You'll want to have a <u>professional photographer</u> who is trained to photograph homes. There are specific details such as which lens to use that are vital. The right lens can make your home look great while providing buyers with an accurate representation of room sizes. If the angle is too wide, buyers will be disappointed when they arrive and see that your home is smaller than they thought. Too narrow a lens gives the impression that the rooms are smaller than they actually are, so they may choose to not even come see your home in person. Real estate photography is an art. You can't just buy a nice camera and take a few photos and expect to compete with similar homes that are photographed by a specialist.

The team should also include someone, perhaps the photographer, who can help you create a virtual tour of your home. Most real estate websites have a link to a virtual tour now. Buyers love this feature because it makes them feel as if they're in the home, without even visiting it. Also, they typically include a lot more photos than are allowed on most websites.

Most top teams have a <u>Marketing Coordinator</u> who follows up with all of the agents and buyers that look at their properties.

They obtain feedback, good or bad, to determine what may be necessary to help sell a particular home. Sometimes this means making a particular offer like a carpet allowance. Other times this might mean a repair like a loose fence board or broken gate latch. This specialist is also tasked with finding out what might influence the buyer who saw the home to make an offer. The Marketing Coordinator is vital in the process; they are actively working to sell a property.

Inside Sales Associates are another key member of the real estate marketing team. They are licensed agents that prospect via telephone calling neighbors of newly or soon-to-be listed homes. Inside Sales Associates ask neighbors if they know of any friends or family who might be interested in moving to the area. This process allows agents to announce that a home is on the market and find potential buyers. This is a form of active marketing in contrast to passive marketing, such as the "Three P Marketing Plan" referenced earlier.

Buyer agents are the final members of an effective marketing team. They are called on to work with buyers only. Interestingly, 9-percent of all buyers find their home and purchase it as a result of a yard sign or open house according the National Association of Realtors®. To capitalize on this, the phone number on each yard sign should call a few buyer agents at the same time to make sure that their call gets answered. This system ensures that buyers will speak to a live person who will answer their questions, get them into the home for a showing, and even assist them in buying the home if it's the one they choose. Without such a method, the buyers who make this call may move on to the next home if their call is not answered.

When the time comes to sell your home you will be faced with crucial decisions as from when to list your home to what your list price should be. These decisions may seem daunting without the help of an expert. The path to successfully selling your home starts with a Realtor® who is willing to share their track record of success and expertise with you, and ends with team of real estate professionals who are poised and ready to help you get top dollar for your home.

About Shawn

Shawn Culhane is a Real Estate Broker and team leader who specializes in the sale of all residential property, including luxury and waterfront properties. Shawn's background includes experience in the construction and engineering fields – which allows him to see things from a different perspective than most agents, while leading a team of marketing specialists.

Shawn is one of Texas' top real estate agents with almost $60M in sales volume from 170 homes in 2014, with plans for over 300 sales in 2015. This ranks him well within the top 1% of all agents locally and nationwide. He was named one of *REALTOR® Magazine's* "30 under 30" award recipients for 2013, a one-time national level award from the National Association of Realtors. In addition, he is a Luxury Home Marketing Specialist and holds the coveted Million Dollar Guild designation, awarded for experience in the $1M+ market.

Shawn's honors and awards are representative of his hard work, integrity, and level of success in helping his clients buy and sell homes. Shawn and his team of marketing professionals have a proven track record when it comes to helping their clients achieve top dollar while selling their homes – and they can help you, too. If you're planning to buy or sell property in Texas, be sure you're working with Culhane Premier Properties by calling 512-686-3862 or sending an email to shawn@shawnculhane.com.

CHAPTER 15

THE CONFLUENCE OF FACTORS IN A REAL ESTATE LISTING DETERMINES YOUR HOME'S TOP DOLLAR — FROM INFORMATION TO IMPLEMENTATION

BY REEM TRAHAN

Not that long ago, people relied on one source for real estate information – their real estate agent. Today, the Internet offers myriad choices for real estate research. Information found on websites like Zillow, Trulia, and Realtor.com should be carefully researched. These companies are in the business of collecting and selling your name. Information such as the "Zestimate®" uses heuristic techniques that find a quick solution which is not guaranteed to be optimal, but good enough for the goal of giving accessible information with a simple click. These strategies, using readily accessible though loosely applicable information to the public, shouldn't be believed without proper research.

Realtors® have rich, more accurate and regulated data one cannot find on the Internet. They have access to accurate, critical and real-time data to share with you, so you don't have to waste your time. Their valuation approach is one that exhausts many sources to make sure their decisions are sound and that their recommendations are reliable.

MY SECRET TO SUCCESS – "TRUTH, PLAIN AND SIMPLE."

I'll never forget when a neighbor invited me to their home to discuss their selling options. Their home was in mint condition, the upgrades they chose were accurate, the home would sell quickly, but we still had to consider the price the market could bear. The couple shared with me the price point they desired. And while I wished very much that I could guarantee selling it at their price, I had to tell them the truth. Keeping a positive but realistic candor is key at this point. I would not put a family through the sometimes arduous listing process, if I didn't believe the house could sell at that price. I shared with them the Competitive Market Analysis (CMA) and showed them what comparable homes were selling for. They thanked me for my time and shared they were interviewing other Realtors®.

A few weeks later, the home was on the market by a different agent. It was a top-producing agent, who is very proficient at creating a CMA and knows well the market. He listed it at the price they desired. Now concerned that I may have failed at nurturing a positive Agent-Client relationship, I reviewed my CMA again, to make sure I hadn't missed any variable. And as I watched the house sit on the market for 3 months, I was certain that my advice was sound, based on the tangible and intangible variables I discussed with them. Seeing my neighbor, after the listing had been withdrawn, I asked her if they were still considering a move. She said that the only way they could have moved was if they received the net from selling it at the price they wanted. And she thanked me for not wasting their time and giving them false hope. This further solidified my philosophy of providing my clients the "truth, plain and simple."

Don't hesitate to contact a Realtor®, even if you just started thinking about selling. The first conversation is not a commitment, but merely there to confirm the possibility. Even if the timing isn't right for you now, at least you have a better idea of when in the future it can become a reality.

SOME TIPS I SUGGEST TO CLIENTS SEEKING A REALTOR®

Perhaps the most important step should be to interview and hire the best Realtor® in your market. The Realtor® you choose should not only make the home-selling process easier for you, but they should help you make smart decisions that will in turn make the sale of your home quick, profitable and smooth.

I have chosen to use Realtor® versus Real Estate Agent throughout this chapter, because a Realtor® is a member of the National Association of REALTORS®, which means that he or she must uphold the standards of the association and its code of ethics. The more education and experience a Realtor® has obtained through their years of practicing, the better they will represent you.

TWELVE QUESTIONS TO ASK WHEN CHOOSING YOUR REALTOR®

1. **How long have you been in residential real estate sales? Is it your full-time job?** While experience is no guarantee of skill, real estate — like many other professions — is mostly learned on the job.

2. **What designations do you hold?** Designations such as GRI and CRS®, which require that agents take additional, specialized real estate training, are held only by about one-quarter of real estate practitioners.

3. **How many homes did you and your real estate brokerage sell last year?** By asking this question, you'll get a good idea of how much experience the practitioner has.

4. **How many days did it take you to sell the average home?** How did that compare to the overall market? The REALTOR® you interview should have these facts on hand, and be able to present market statistics from the local MLS to provide a comparison.

5. **How close to the initial asking prices of the homes you sold were the final sale prices?** This is one indication of how skilled the REALTOR® is at pricing homes and marketing to suitable buyers. Of course, other factors also may be at play, including an exceptionally hot or cool real estate market.

6. **What types of specific marketing systems and approaches will you use to sell my home?** You don't want someone who's going to put a For Sale sign in the yard and hope for the best. Look for someone who has aggressive and innovative approaches, and knows how to market your property competitively on the Internet. Buyers today want information fast, so it's important that your REALTOR® is responsive.

7. **Will you represent me exclusively, or will you represent both the buyer and the seller in the transaction?** While it's usually legal to represent both parties in a transaction, it's important to understand where the practitioner's obligations lie. Your REALTOR® should explain his or her agency relationship to you and describe the rights of each party.

8. **Can you recommend service providers who can help me obtain a mortgage, make home repairs, and help with other things I need done?** Because REALTORS® are immersed in the industry, they're wonderful resources as you seek lenders, home improvement companies, and other home service providers. Practitioners should generally recommend more than one provider and let you know if they have any special relationship with or receive compensation from any of the providers.

9. **What type of support and supervision does your brokerage office provide to you?** Having resources such as in-house support staff, access to a real estate attorney, and assistance with technology can help an agent sell your home.

10. **What's your business philosophy?** While there's no right answer to this question, the response will help you assess what's important to the agent and determine how closely the agent's goals and business emphasis mesh with your own.

11. **How will you keep me informed about the progress of my transaction? How frequently?** Again, this is not a question with a correct answer, but how you judge the response will reflect your own desires. Do you want updates twice a week or do you prefer not to be bothered unless there's a hot prospect? Do you prefer phone, e-mail, or a personal visit?

12. **Could you please give me the names and phone numbers of your three most recent clients?** Ask recent clients if they would work with this REALTOR® again. Find out whether they were pleased with the communication style, follow-up, and work ethic of the REALTOR®.

In addition to asking your Realtor® questions, the questions your Realtor® asks you are just as important.

QUESTIONS YOUR REALTOR® SHOULD ASK YOU

In addition to you asking the right questions, your Realtor® should also be asking you the right questions. For instance:

* Why do you want to sell?
* How much are your underlying loans?
* What special features does the home include?
* Are you interested in remodeling or updating?

- Is the purchase of a new home subject to the sale of the current home?

- If the home is not vacant, what is your preferred criteria and method for scheduling showings? Text message, email, phone call? Advance notice?

The Realtor® should be taking Detailed *notes of your responses.*

DON'T FORGET THIS CONVERSATION ABOUT DUAL AGENCY!

A very important conversation that your Realtor® should have with you before you sign the Listing Agreement is "Dual Agency." It's legal in my state of Virginia, but I will never engage in "dual agency." This is the act of representing buyers AND sellers in the same transaction. I think you deserve an exclusive representation. It's very important to understand what happens to the relationship with your Realtor®, if you allow dual agency to come into play.

Important Tip!

While commissions are always negotiable, be careful of the Realtor® who is quick to drop their commission to gain your business. If the Realtor® cannot negotiate his own commission, how well can they negotiate Top Dollar for your home?

You've made the decision to sell your home and you've chosen the most professional and trusted Realtor®. Now it's time to decide on a List Price. It's understandable that sellers want to realize the highest possible price from their real estate. However, over improvements, a seller's enthusiasm, or their emotional attachment may prompt Sellers to list above market value or turn down offers below their asking price. Most people shopping for real estate know what comparable homes are selling for. Pricing it right from the start avoids appraisal problems, loan rejections and lost time. There are many factors that are used when pricing a home.

PRICING TIPS FOR MY CLIENTS

1. **Price your home based on the following**: Active Homes (these homes will be your competition), Under Contract Homes (these will eventually settle and be comparables, or may come back on the market as competition), and Sold Homes (these will be used in the appraisal report). Your Realtor® should go and view the Active homes on the market that compare to yours. I have had some clients attend these viewings. View them as if you were a buyer.

2. **Get a Pre-listing home inspection:** Having your home inspection before a buyer is interested, makes you better informed. This gives you control of issues that are found and gets you a higher return on your investment.

3. **Get your home photo-shoot ready:** The exterior is very important! Inside, the key word is clean. Remove clutter, organize and depersonalize. Some clients need me to put together a to-do list for them. Some clients require the advice of a professional decorator to help them budget a renovation, small or large.

4. **Professional Photos & Videos:** Great shots of your home are a must! 90% of homebuyers begin their search online. Many buyers share their disappointment with me about the listing photos being advertised online. They skip homes based on their photos, before even reading through the details. If your Realtor® is not an expert photographer, then make sure they hire one.

5. **Marketing**: You want your house to explode onto the market!!!

   • **Coming Soon** listings are great, as they generate interest early on. I've had buyers who were about to make an offer on a property, but after a Coming Soon listing appeared, they waited to make certain their decision was best.

- Your Realtor® should utilize an **aggressive mix of online vehicles** to maximize exposure of your property to the public and to the brokerage community. Top sites include Zillow, Trulia, Listingbook, Military by Owner offer enhanced listings to ensure your house is top and center. There are additional charges associated with marketing with these sites, and you want to ensure your Realtor® has a budget equipped to market your listing.

- Your Realtor® should **advertise** to their friends, agents and neighbors, every chance they get through flyers, Internet ads, signs, postcards, and word-of-mouth.

6. **Agent Initial Contact:** Ensure your Realtor® lists state that Buyers Agents should contact Listing Agent before showing, even when the property is vacant. This allows your Realtor® the opportunity to connect with the prospective Buyers Agent. Exciting details about your home can be discussed, as well as other pertinent information. This also allows your Realtor® to gently learn more about the potential buyer.

7. **Showing Management Technology or a System:** Your Realtor® should have a system in place that date and time logs everyone who has entered the property, utilizing the lockbox. This system will also send out an automatic feedback request from every agent who visits your home, and once the agent completes it, sends it to myself and my client. If no feedback is received within a day, the Realtor® should make a follow-up call to see if they had any questions about the showing and gather information.

8. **For Sale Sign**: Make sure the For Sale sign stands out and looks nice. Make sure there are enough directional signs for more buyers to find your house.

9. **Open House:** I don't necessarily feel that Open Houses get your home sold, I will hold them for clients who want them. Most motivated buyers are working with a Realtor®

and have been financially approved to make a purchase in the range they are viewing. Most people coming through the doors of an Open House are neighbors curious about your house, people who are just starting looking, but not ready, or people who are excited to buy now, but haven't started the loan process.

10. **Direct Phone:** You should be able to connect directly with your Realtor® when it's important. It can be very frustrating if you are passed off to other team members who don't know the situation well, and you have to give them the history to get an answer.

11. **Reviewing & Comparing Offers:** Don't discard low offers. Think of them as an interested buyer who wants to negotiate for one reason or another. A seller should respond and be gracious, say the offer doesn't fit their needs, and make a counteroffer. It's not always about price. You have to take into consideration that timelines, contingencies, lender, loan-type, earnest money deposit, can be just as important as the purchase price.

CLOSING THOUGHTS

Selling property is much more than just sticking a sign in the ground! . . . Or searching the Internet. Even in the best of markets, a Realtor® with proven results will ensure a hassle-free, smooth transaction. Their ability to analyze market trends, interpret sales data and accurately price properties is very essential. Your Realtor® should customize their marketing program for your individual property. And most importantly, keep you informed about next steps, ways to save time and money, and ways to avoid stress throughout the process. Realizing that good home pricing is a blend of art and science and having an experienced professional Realtor® familiar with the local market in your area will help ensure you get the best deal possible.

About Reem

Reem Trahan's story is one of balance and perseverance through adversity and success. Reem has, during the past 15 years, seamlessly switched focus between being a mother of 4 children and growing a top-producing real estate business in Northern Virginia. Her passion for both has helped her to excel, between supporting her daughters' competitive sports and providing her clients top-notch customer service by demonstrating her tireless dedication to their real-estate needs. A role model for her children and her profession, she has instilled in her children the narrative of a success story, through which in spite of myriad ups and downs she has prevailed, and continues to excel. Her children approach academics, sports and life with the same vigor and enthusiasm Reem shows in her every-day existence. And for this she is proud.

Reem demonstrates her excellence in customer service as a top-notch Realtor® daily, and has been awarded the NVAR Multi-Million Dollar Sales Club Award, REMAX 100% Club and REMAX Platinum Club – as well as making it on the REMAX Mid-Atlantic Region Top Producer List (#9, as of May 2014). In fact, Reem has positioned herself to be one of the top 1% of real estate agents in Northern Virginia.

Reem's passion for real estate grew from advice she once provided her mother on a property. Instead of selling the property and taking a loss, Reem advised her to hold and rent the property to later sell it, tripling her profit. Later when Reem was looking to purchase a new home, her friend and Realtor® convinced her to learn the business to better address the complex calculus involved with the purchase of a new home. Turmoil followed in Reem's life, which allowed her to rediscover her passions – learning about real estate and caring for her children. During this period, she worked for a prestigious homebuilder and developer in the new construction division, and she learned many important skills, which would serve her well later on.

Through her exposure in the real estate industry, she was able to quickly learn the business of building, buying, selling and flipping homes. But she needed more. In 2004, after earning her professional real estate license, she continued completing many hours of coursework that is not required, but adds value for her clients. All the while, as a single mother she was raising quickly growing children, and honing her real estate skills. She continues to stay up-to-date on current trends in the industry by attending classes, seminars, and conferences. She best serves her clients by meeting their needs, their budgets, and most importantly – by keeping them positive and energized throughout the sometimes onerous process of buying, selling and investing in a home. Reem's success through adversity and personal turmoil has molded her into the expert Realtor® she has become. And although she has accomplished so much, she will never stop learning so that she will always bring value to her clients in this ever-changing world of Real Estate.

Reem is grateful for her supportive husband, Donnie, who has always believed in her. She is inspired by her amazing daughters, Jenna, Aiyah, Giselle and Milan on their hard work, dedication, persistence, and how they respond positively to setbacks and failure!

CHAPTER 16

THE REAL ESTATE SYSTEM IS BROKEN

BY JEREMY BACK

THE REAL ESTATE SYSTEM IS BROKEN

There is inadequate training and no real-life experience required to become a licensed real estate agent to handle your most valuable asset, your home. For an individual to become a licensed real estate agent, they simply need to spend 120 hours in real estate school. This is 1,880 less hours than what is required for the person who cuts your hair. Most agents opt to take this schooling online which includes watching a recording of an instructor teaching about rules, ethics, and laws. Never does an agent receive any training on how to effectively market a home and ensure that the home is selling for *top dollar*. Nor is there a requirement for any real world experience prior to receiving a license. This is why agents with about as much market and marketing experience as yourself, and inadequate training or knowledge, surround you the homeowner. Unfortunately, they are trying to make thousands of dollars off the commission of your home that you have been investing in for years.

These average agents spend less than $89 per month on their business expenses and on marketing listed properties. Because they have little or no money invested into your home and hardly any training, their first response to your home not selling is "We need to reduce the price," or pressure you to take an offer that is far less than the listed price. They may have invested $89 compared to your many thousands of dollars, and the only consequence to them is a couple of hundred dollars less in commission – when compared to your thousands of dollars lost on your investment.

One of the main reasons for this broken system is that the average agent doesn't understand what their job is. If you ask any real estate agent, most of them will tell you that their job is to sell your home. But that is not the job; that is actually the outcome of doing their job. An agent's job is to drive the market to your home, and obtain as much money as possible for the sale of your home. Moreover, agents will learn and understand your goals and real estate needs in order to appropriately advise you. This is accomplished through agents thoroughly understanding the market in your residential area. Because agents believe that the result is their job, the only tool your average agent has is to lower the price of your home at every corner until it is sold. Meanwhile, the agent is still going to make thousands of dollars on your home while you are left with no equity. Price is an important part, but it is just one-step of many in order to sell your home for *top dollar*.

DOES THE FOLLOWING SOUND FAMILIAR?

You decide that it is time to move, so you list your home with a real estate agent. The agent brings you a CMA (Comparative Market Analysis), which includes some prior data of homes comparative to yours that have sold in your area. Next, the agent will recommend the price that you should sell your biggest investment for. This agent never asks why you are selling, what you hope to accomplish with this sale or anything about you, they only talk about themselves and how they can sell your home. They have no idea who your competition is and what the absorption rate is for your house. If you get lucky they might even have some stats for the county or area. You, the homeowner, have a price in your head for what you want to get for your home, and although the price data the agent shared with you doesn't match the price in your head, the agent agrees to list your home at that price without a second thought. Why would the agent do this? The agent is desperate to get your business and will tell you anything in the beginning to get it. They may even agree to lower their commission to get your listing. The average agent sells less then 4 homes a year.

"Did you know that agents can borrow money from lenders on homes they have under contract before the deal closes on your home?"

Once the agent has your listing, they will take some pictures of your home and post those online with the big sites such as Zillow, Realtor.com, Trulia.com, etc. as well as the Multiple Listing Service (MLS). They put a sign in your yard and create a flyer to put next to the sign. Then you wait. Meanwhile, the agent is getting calls on your home from potential buyers. However, they are not trying to exclusively sell your home, but get additional clients and listings. They use your listing to attract other potential clients, and hope that other agents will notice your home and have clients that will want to see it. Remember: the agent only has a monthly business budget of $89 a month, so they need *your* house, to get *new* business. Agents are taught to use their listing inventory as a main way to drive in business. You would think an agent's focus would be to sell your home. That's why you hired them in the first place, isn't it?

As you can tell, this process does not work, so after a few weeks on the market, your agent returns and asks you to lower the price around 5-10% to see if that will generate more interest. Over and over you drop your price until it finally sells a year later, and you have no equity left in your home. You end up selling your greatest investment for a lot less than you ever thought, and the process was so stressful for so long, that you swear to never sell a home again. Many times the home doesn't sell at all during the listing period. In this market, almost 50% of all the homes listed end up not selling during the time of the listing contract.

HOW DO WE FIX THIS MESS?

How does the consumer protect themselves from these average agents that are everywhere? The answer is simple: the homeowner needs to seek out agents that are *Top Dollar Agents*.

A Top Dollar Agent is someone that invests in his or her client's home and has a large marketing budget dedicated to selling that home. You have invested thousands of dollars into your home. Your agent should be willing to do the same to ensure it sells for top dollar. A Top Dollar Agent is someone who continues their education not only regarding the Real Estate Industry, but who also takes classes to learn best practices in sales and negotiations from other industries. These agents know how to build a business and they will have a dedicated team with specific job functions to sell your home. Their team focus will be to help you meet your goals, to market your home and do everything the agent can possibly do before they ask you to reduce the price of your home. A Top Dollar Agent will not list a home that they do not believe they can sell with the predetermined expectations they have discussed with you. A top agent will be honest with you and give you real data no matter the end result. You and your priorities, driving the qualified buyers to your home, and helping negotiate top dollar for you, is what a Top Dollar Agent and their team should be focused on.

HOW DO YOU FIND A TOP DOLLAR AGENT?

You take the time to research agents such as the Jeremy Back Home Selling Team. You look for agents who are trained and are experts in selling homes for top dollar. For the Jeremy Back Home Selling Team, we train daily on the best sales strategies and are constantly monitoring pricing as well as supply and demand in your area. After 25 combined years in the industry, we have learned how to effectively market your home and use other offers besides price, to get the buyers to your home. We know how to price your home to compete with the local market and how to proactively attract qualified buyers to your home. We review daily metrics and stats that are required to inform you on what the market is doing and where the buyers are. We have created a pricing strategy to keep more money in your pocket when your home sells.

Last. and most importantly, we invest thousands of dollars to market your home and ensure that your home sells quickly and for *top dollar*. We are invested, just like you, in the sale of your home. We are focused, just like you, to ensure we get top dollar for that investment. We are able to do this because we understand how to attract buyers that are qualified, to the homes we sell. We have a dedicated team with specific roles, and everyone is held personally accountable for the selling of your home. We are transparent and creative in the process, so that you can always know what your bottom line is and see what we are doing to get *you* top dollar.

We will not ask you to lower your price until we believe 100% that we have done everything we can do to drive the market to your home. As your Real Estate Team, we will advise you and give you information on what market indicators could help or hurt your sales price in the future – like changes to lending practices, competition, absorption rates, and interest rates. We provide you with the feedback from every person who sees your home including the price they felt would have driven them to your home.

Before you hire another agent . . . ask the following questions:

- How much money will you spend to market my home?
- How will that money be spent to drive buyers to my home?
- May I see examples of what your Real Estate Team is doing right now to attract buyers to other homes?

- May I see a marketing plan for my home so I will be able to ensure that your Real Estate Team is following that plan?

- What education and training has your Real Estate Team done, or are pursuing, to strategically learn best practices and new standards for selling homes for *top dollar*?

To fix this broken system, we need you, the homeowner, to hire the Top Dollar agents that are willing to market, train, and continually work (full time) to help clients achieve their goals. Over and over we have been told that more Americans build wealth through real estate than any other method. It is time to protect that wealth and align with the Jeremy Back Home Selling Team . . . and other top dollar agents who understand this, and are continuously learning and applying the best practices for getting you, the homeowner, *TOP DOLLAR*.

About Jeremy

Jeremy Back was raised in Bountiful, Utah, the oldest son of a Real Estate investor, entrepreneur and a schoolteacher. Jeremy enrolled in the Air Force as a young adult, where he had the privilege of being an Air Traffic Controller and was stationed at Hill Air Force Base in Layton, Utah, which was very close to home. Upon completing his service and being honorably discharged from the military, Jeremy pursued Real Estate and has been licensed for over 11 years as a top-producing agent. In that time, he has developed and sold hundreds of lots, and has marketed new construction, investment properties, flip homes, bank-owned homes and foreclosures.

Jeremy has worked with hundreds of homeowners to get top dollar for their home by understanding the market better than most other agents. Jeremy really understands where the buyers are, and how to drive those buyers to his clients' homes through strategic marketing and training with top marketers and sales companies – not only in the real estate industry, but outside of the industry as well, with people like Jay Abraham.

Jeremy is a strong advocate for success as a team and not just as an individual. He has structured the Jeremy Back Home Selling Team to have high standards of customer service, integrity, and constant training. This creative vision and attitude for success shatters the competition and creates a close relationship with his clients who continue to use his expertise, as well as give him referrals. Jeremy has won the respect of his colleagues and clients as he persists in his dedication to helping others. He is truly one of the best in the business and there is simply no substitute for his passion and dedication.

Jeremy has been married to the love of his life for over 11 years and he and his wife, Lindsey, have three beautiful children.

CHAPTER 17

HOW TO HIRE A LISTING AGENT

BY BRENT GOVE

You are likely about to sell your most valuable possession! You will use the proceeds to fund your retirement or potentially parlay some of the profits into other lucrative investments. After buying and selling Real Estate for almost 20 years and participating in 3,000+ real estate transactions, I've seen hopeful homeowners do it all! From the overconfident "for sale by owner" zealot, to the naive and inexperienced homeowner, they list with the first reasonable agent they meet. In fact, 71% of all owners list with the first agent they meet. Wow! Shocking! They hand over the responsibility of selling their family's greatest asset to a total stranger! In this chapter I will share what not to do, what you will be tempted to do and what you should do. So, let's get started!

Mistake Number One: Hire a friend or relative to sell your home. (If something goes terribly wrong...are you going to sue Grandpa or your Sister?)

Mistake Number Two: Hire the first agent you meet while looking at open houses. (I know you like them or you would not have hired them, but are they any good at selling and marketing real estate?)

Mistake Number Three: Hire the agent that sold your house. (Many agents are specialists and are called buyer-agents for a reason. There is a night-and-day different between the job of finding a home and the job of selling a home for the highest possible price within the quickest time frame.)

Mistake Number Four: Hiring your neighbor or a co-worker's spouse to sell your home. (Again, they may look and smell great, but can they get the job done with excellence?)

Here is what you should do. Check around with family, friends, and co-workers for personal referrals to agents they have had wonderful experiences with. Once you have a list of three to five agents from a variety of companies, it's time to get started with the interview process! Have them come to your home and answer the following questions:

1: What's my house worth and why?

2: What are the comparable properties you are using to determine the likely sales price?

3: How many listings have you sold this year?

4: How long have you been in real estate?

5: How many active listings do you have right now?

6: What is your market plan for my house?

7: How long do you estimate it will take to sell my house in the current market?

8: What sets you apart from any other agents I would talk too?

*The last two questions are the most important!

9: How do you handle the appraisal?

10: Can you make a buyer write an offer?

Back to number 9…most agents just let the appraisal happen. In fact, they let the buyer's agent (who may be brand new), open the house for the appraiser. Three to four days later, the appraisal comes in at $10,000, $20,000, or $30,000 under the sales price. The buyer puts his/her foot down and says, "I will pay the appraised value only." (Not one dime over!) Your agent suggests meeting the buyer halfway to try and hold the deal together. He or she suggests you drop $15,000 and the buyer comes up $15,000 over the appraised value. The buyer agrees to this and you think "Wow...I have the greatest agent on planet earth! They just got the buyer to pay $15,000 over the appraised value!" When in fact...just the opposite is true! Your agent lost you $15,000! Your agent should have been at that appraisal appointment. Your agent should have made you type out a list of all home improvements that you have made and the retail dollar amounts of those improvements. For example, you may have personally installed a beautiful redwood deck for $5,000 that a general contractor would have charged $15,000 for. Do not put $5,000 down for the decks value because you are not giving yourself credit for your sweat equity, your labor! Put down the true value of that deck, $15,000.

I have had homeowners tell me that they have easily invested $100,000 into their home, only to build the list and see they had invested $200,000 into their property. I remember when I handed a detailed written list with the dollar amount exceeding $200,000 to the appraiser, who was struggling to justify the sales price, which was $40,000 more than all the comparable properties that could be used, he enthusiastically thanked me. Armed with this detailed list of upgrades, he simply noted the file to justify the higher sales price, because the comparable properties...just weren't comparable! This happens all the time! I believe I saved the client $40,000 dollars! You don't have to pay to get a good agent...it pays to get a good agent!

Remember, you pay for what you get! The reason most discount agents work for 4.5% or 5% vs. 6% to 7% is twofold. Reason one is they've been in the business for a while, maybe 10 or 20 years, and they just aren't getting referral business. So they have to compete for business by lowering their fees. While you may be tempted to save $2,000 or $3,000 in fees, I believe the downside could easily cost you $20,000 or $30,000. Maybe your home sold in a week for $830,000 and you were thrilled – thinking your agent is pure genius! What if it could have sold in three weeks for its true value of $850,000? That's an extra $20,000.

Think about it…you either get a "New" agent who is practicing real estate with your family's greatest asset or you could get a real estate agent who's been around the block and isn't getting referred enough because they aren't any good! The super stars of real estate will charge between 6% and 7%! The rest discount and hope for the best! The general rule is true…you pay for what you get!!

About Brent

Since 1997, Brent Gove has been successfully selling real estate in the Sacramento area, following the example set by his parents, both long-time Real Estate Brokers. He and his team sell hundreds of homes annually, within the Sacramento, Placer, and El Dorado counties.

For over 6 years, Brent has been the local expert and host of "The Real Estate Report with Brent Gove" on Northern California's number one talk radio station KFBK 1530 AM, one of the top 15 AM stations in America.

Brent's new book, *Momentum,* has just been released through Irish Canon Press and is selling rapidly throughout the nation. *Momentum* is a strategic guide to success for Real Estate Agents and Brokers.

Though he started out as a one-man show, Brent started building a full-service team of agents and staff in 2000 to meet the needs of his clients.

Brent's accomplishments include being the C.E.O. and Team Leader of Keller Williams' Roseville, California office. Prior to Keller Williams, he qualified as the #2 RE/MAX Agent in the state of California and #11 RE/MAX Agent in the world out of 128,000 agents! Today, Brent is an International Speaker, Sales Trainer, Author and Business Coach.

Brent states: "By building a team, my agents and I can focus solely on our clients' needs, while our staff focuses on the administrative details involved in each transaction. In addition, we can come together and brainstorm when we face challenges and, of course, encourage the integrity and character of each agent and transaction." His motto is: *ALWAYS DO THE RIGHT THING IN EVERY SITUATION.*

Of all of Brent's accomplishments, he is most proud of being a husband to his beautiful wife Kathy and a Dad to his five children. Outside of the office, he is active in coaching his kids' soccer teams and the family loves to travel. Brent is an avid golfer, and they are very involved in their church.

Brent often says: "One of my favorite things to do is to help a first-time homebuyer. The sense of satisfaction that comes when I hand them the key to their new home is priceless. I guess real estate is just in my blood."

And over 3,000 satisfied clients would have to agree!

CHAPTER 18

THE PROVEN PLAN BEHIND MAXIMIZING YOUR HOME SALES PRICE

BY KRIS BOWEN

When I was a 16-year-old teenager I moved to Las Vegas to stay with some friends. I had $63 in my pocket, and a beat-up 1984 Chevy Cavalier. I wasn't sure what I was looking for, but I wanted an adventure and to find clarity on what I wanted out of life. As I settled in, I became fascinated with computers and a new "thing" called the World Wide Web. I thought it was really fascinating that I could post something online and have someone in another country view it immediately.

As an enterprising 16 year old, I quickly realized the power of what the World Wide Web (Internet) could do as a tool to freely exchange information to the masses. I spent many months learning from my friends and numerous text books on how to program a website. My first website was called KingLink.com and was a repository for free games and software. I built the traffic to my site by telling every other website on the Internet about my site and having them link to me. Within 6 months I had one of the most popular software websites online. I realized the income potential I had with the massive amount of traffic I was experiencing and ended up making $1500 a month selling ads on my website. This was huge in 1995, especially for a 16 year old, and a game changer for me personally!

The Internet was becoming popular and I jumped into building websites for many businesses. In 1995, I programmed one of the very first e-commerce sites on the Internet. This website bought and sold used CDs online (they are still in business today). After my success helping build a business, I started creating many other websites and became a master at online marketing. I've designed web applications for many Fortune 100 companies including Intel®, Microsoft®, HP®, Symantec® and Novell® among others.

In 2003, I realized I had a passion for sales and marketing and made the jump into real estate sales. I sold my IT Company and started my real estate career full time. The real estate industry was late to the technology game and this provided a great opportunity for me. I knew that if I built a website that had the consumer in mind it would be successful. In 2005, I launched a website: zoomUTAH.com which quickly became one of the most popular websites in Utah to find a home. Today the website has over 55,000 registered members and growing every day.

I've built many businesses during the past years, some of them more profitable than others, but I learned something profound from each one of them. The common variable in my most successful businesses was having a clear objective and plan in place. Selling a home is no different and is a complex process that needs a clear objective and plan.

Every home has unique characteristics that will either appeal to, or deter, different Buyers. Depending on what desired features your home presents to each buyer will determine the price the buyer is willing to pay for your home. Creating a mini business plan will help you identify what unique features your home possesses, who your ideal buyer is, and how to reach a buyer willing to pay you *Top Dollar*! Just like when you are looking to sell a business, you want to position the company so that any potential buyers see the maximum opportunity that they could realize if they wrote you a check to buy your business.

In order to maximize the sales price on your home, you need to outline the following categories:

1. Description
2. SWOT Analysis
   (Strengths, Weaknesses, Opportunities & Threats)
3. Competitor Analysis
4. Sold Market Analysis
5. Positioning
6. Marketing Plan
7. Desired Result

Do these categories sound familiar? These same categories directly relate to an effective business plan. I utilize this plan in each and every home that I list. Let me show you this plan in action on a home that I recently closed in 1 day for well over the asking price. The demonstration below is a shortened version of an actual plan.

1. Description: *"Enjoy coming home to this 5 bedroom, 3 bathroom Ranch/Rambler located in one of Sandy's best neighborhoods. This wonderful home features hardwood floors, wood burning fireplace, master bathroom with walk-in closet, two family rooms, spacious rooms, lots of storage, RV parking, fully fenced yard, covered deck. Walk to Eastridge Park!"*

2. SWOT Analysis:

Strengths
What are the strong selling points to this home? Many bedrooms, great location, master closet and bathroom, RV Parking, close to great schools and a park.

Weaknesses

What are some of the less desirable features of this home? Side of home is on a main road, wood shake shingles (not common in my area), small lot, needs updating, comparable homes have a 3-car garage.

Opportunities

What opportunities does this home offer a buyer? Update the home for instant equity, high appreciation area, ideal for a buyer that has use for all of the bedrooms and for the RV pad, prefers a single-level home.

Threats

What outside threats will I encounter when trying to sell this home? Comparable homes are updated inside, a lot of competition on the market, slow time of year for sales, seller must sell quickly.

3. **Competitor Analysis**: Nine comparable homes active on the market with an "average days on market" of 57 days. I was able to speak to four listing agents on the comparable properties and found that their showing activity has been on average one to two buyers per week. I feel only two of the comparable homes were properly marketed and presented well to attract buyers.

4. **Sold Market Analysis:** One comparable home is in escrow ready to close, three comparable homes have sold in the last 90 days with an average sold price per square foot of $88. If there were no other comparable homes added to the market starting today, how many days would it take for the market to absorb the inventory? Understanding this figure will help you determine how long your home may be on the market.

5. **Positioning:**

   • **Understand your Ideal Buyer:** Objective is to occupy a clear, unique, and advantageous position in the consumer's mind. How can we position this home on the market to attract the highest possible sales price? The ideal buyer for this home would have use for all five bedrooms. They would be interested in updating the home to increase its value; having the schools and park nearby is a big plus, and they don't want to deal with a lot of yard maintenance.

- **Price Positioning:** The As-Is value of home is around $260k. 93% of buyers search online for homes, so optimizing this listing online is crucial. I always try to price a home to fit inside $25k price brackets. Example: $200k, $225k, $250k, etc. I also know that in my market, the most common price point buyers are looking at is between $225k and $250k. If I price the home at $260k, the home will be competing against homes at $275k and will often be overlooked by prospective buyers. To maximize interest in this home, I want to price this home at $250k and push to drive the ultimate sales price over the $260k value by encouraging a multiple-offer situation.

- **Presentation:** Ask yourself, when my ideal buyer walks in my front door, what is the best way I can present my home to this person. If you are not skilled in interior design there are many professionals out there that do a fantastic job and can help you position your home to present itself in the best light. This may include moving furniture, removing clutter, de-personalizing the home by taking down photos, adding furniture, painting, etc.

6. **Marketing Plan:** I won't outline my entire marketing plan in this book, but I can tell you it is well over 150 steps. Each listing goes through the same step-by-step process, but the way you target your ideal buyer within each of the platforms (Facebook, Google, etc.), will differ. Narrow down your audience to buyers that would be a perfect fit for your home.

7. **Desired Result:** You must be clear from the beginning with an outline of not only how to get your desired result but what does the win look like. What would it take for you to feel it was a success? It may be about the highest sales price, a fast closing or many other reasons. Whatever it is, you need to know what your desired result is up front.

The seller wanted to sell their home for $260k, which was fair market value for the home, and close fast so they can move on with their life. The plan of action was clear on how we were going to achieve this, and we painted a picture of what success looks like in the end.

So you may be wondering, what was the result with this listing after we posted it for sale on the market? When we hit the market this home was one of the best-priced homes in the area and we ended up with 14 showings the very first day. Keep in mind this was a slow time of year in my market. Out of the 14 showings, we ended up with 9 offers, of which several were over the $250k list price. In the end, we settled at a sales price of $275k with a strong buyer and we successfully closed on the home in three weeks. We over-achieved our goals and the seller has an extra $15k in their pocket because of a well-thought-out plan.

We treat your home as a valuable product. In order to sell your product for the highest price we help you find your target customer and how to achieve your desired result. Indiscriminate action is not an effective way to produce desired results. Selling one of the largest assets most people will ever own is serious business – and we treat it like one.

About Kris

As a native of the Salt Lake Valley, Kris Bowen has worked as a licensed Real Estate professional in Utah since 2003. Kris has turned his years of experience as a successful entrepreneur and previous business owner in the technology sector, into a vehicle for helping Buyers and Sellers.

In 2004, Kris built zoomUTAH.com, Utah's #1 Real Estate website. Since it's launch, zoomUTAH.com has exploded on the local scene. With over 55,000 registered Buyers & Sellers, it has become the website for researching real estate in Utah. The website has allowed Kris to expose his listings to more Buyers as well as provide a platform for Buyers to start their search for Utah real estate.

Although these services give his clients an edge, nothing compares to the personal service, constant communication and commitment that he believes is essential in being successful in this business.

Kris has been featured in numerous local and national TV broadcasts, radio shows, written two books and is recognized as Utah's go-to real estate expert in educating the public about the local Utah real estate market.

Kris knows marketing and has a proven, repeatable system to successfully close on a home for top dollar. Kris' team is composed of marketing gurus that have given his Seller-clients a major advantage in reaching the largest number of potential Buyers. To put things in perspective, the average agent invested $1,070* in marketing. Last year, the Kris Bowen Real Estate Team invested **$217,811!**

Notable facts:

- Kris' team is in the Top 1% in closed volume in Utah
- 2014 Salt Lake Board #1 Small Team of the Year Award Winner!
- Out of over 2,000 real estate agents nationwide, Kris' team was ranked #1 in real estate sales for Equity Real Estate in 2014

- Kris' dynamic team includes:
  - Dedicated Home Selling Expert Advisor
  - Five Dedicated Home Buyer Expert Advisors
  - Client Care Coordinator
  - Transaction Coordinator
  - Professional Photographer/Videographer
  - Professional Interior Designer
  - Team Coach & Mentor
  - Two Online Marketing Consultants
  - Content Writer
  - Web Programmer

- Kris Bowen is the author of two books:

  - *Top Dollar* - the top strategies used by the world's top real estate agents on how to maximize the sales price of their listings. Hardback and digital books will be available Summer 2015 distributed by Ingram Books, and will be available to bookstores nationwide.

  - *What to Know Before Buying or Selling a Home in Salt Lake* - the ultimate resource for homebuyers and sellers in the Salt Lake market. Available on Amazon.com, Barnes & Noble, Apple's iBookstore, as well as other fine bookstores. ISBN: 978-1-62535-600-0

- 5-Star Rating on Zillow.com and many other verified review sites

- National Speaker & Mentor for other real estate professionals around North America

- Their Home Buyer Expert Advisors can successfully get the seller to pay for your closing costs over 95% of the time

- Having a team allows them to be available when you need them

- When you purchase or sell your home with their team, they contribute a portion of their commissions to the Shriners Hospitals for Children®

Kris Bowen lives in Draper, Utah with his wife Kelly, and his two daughters – Brecklyn and Kaslin.

* Data provided by the 2012 National Association of Realtors® Member Survey

CHAPTER 19

PREPARING YOUR HOME FOR SALE

BY MICHAEL KINAR

One of the biggest problems I see in the real estate industry is the lack of preparation that usually goes into preparing a home for sale before it hits the market, even though it is of utmost importance.

A perfect example of this is a couple who I recently assisted with the sale of their home. Pat and Grace had previously listed their home for sale with a typical real estate agent. Pat and Grace had their home up for sale for four months, with no offers coming in and very few potential buyers even booking appointments to look at it. The biggest concern for Pat and Grace was that they really wanted to be situated in a new home before winter; they had health issues which made looking after their large property challenging, especially contending with the snow that comes in winter.

After meeting with Pat and Grace and doing an expired listing analysis, I realized why they were having challenges attracting interest in the home, which ultimately prevented it from selling. The issue I found is all too common in the real estate industry; lack of preparation prior to bringing the home to the market. Pat and Grace's previous real estate agent met with them, did not give them any pointers in preparing their home for sale, and took a number of subpar photos with the camera on his phone (not to mention many duplicates, photos from the same angle and poor lighting).

Our process is entirely different. I initially met with Pat and Grace to look at their property as well as conduct a Seller Counselling Interview to determine their timing, needs and motivation. From there, we utilized our Expert Advisor Home Selling System and the power of differentiation to obtain the results that Pat and Grace were looking for.

Simply put, differentiation is what drives consumer preference and can help a property sell for more money. If your home has the same subpar photos and bland property description as many other listings, it will get lost in a sea of mediocrity and will not stand out amongst the competition. Having an effective differentiation strategy can help a property sell for up to 3 to 5% more money.

Specifically referring to preparing their home to sell, we outlined seven specific strategies to differentiate Pat and Grace's home. They were:

1. Expert Staging Advice

We employ a professional stager to meet with all of our home-selling clients. Our stager spends 30 to 60 minutes with our clients and provides recommendations and suggestions in regards to preparing their home for sale. This process is mostly about working with what they have. For example repositioning furniture, de-cluttering a busy house, some minor painting, etc. Having a home professionally staged dramatically increases the odds of it selling. It also decreases the time on market by up to 50%. It also results in higher offers, as it increases the perceived value. The approximate return on investment is 250 to 500%.

In Pat and Grace's case, the stager's main focus was de-cluttering the house. Pat and Grace had a large home, but it was full of more furniture than you might expect in a house of that size. They also had many personal items and trinkets on display throughout their home. Utilizing the stager's advice, Pat and Grace cleared much of their excess furniture out of the house and removed most of the personal items and trinkets. The result was immediately noticeable; their home seemed much larger and spacious. Removing the personal items and trinkets was also beneficial because, as potential buyers started coming through the home, they were able to focus on the house without distractions and picture it as their own home.

2. Quality-Of-Life Upgrade Analysis
In this strategy we work with the stager, our contractor and the home owner to evaluate possible upgrades that substantially increase the value of the home. This is a professionally-managed process in which we try to help the client achieve the lowest price on the completed work. This process increases the perceived value, and also drives up demand against strong competition. During this process, we have to be target-market focused. For example, we would not recommend a client put in granite counter tops if they are in an area and price range in which the target market is first-time home buyers.

Our Quality-Of-Life Upgrade Analysis indicated that the area we could most substantially increase the value of Pat and Grace's home was in repainting some rooms. Pat and Grace had a few rooms in the house which were painted in bright and bold colors. We encouraged them to allow our contractor to repaint these rooms in soft earth tones. The result was neutral colors throughout the house, which could appeal to all potential buyers and more easily allow them to visualize their furniture and belongings in the home.

3. Professional Pre-Inspection
During this process, we have our home inspector visit the home and conduct a full professional pre-inspection. The pre-inspection will identify potential major deal killers

and high "return on investment" repairs. It is much more beneficial for us to discover potential deal killers at this point, rather than have a buyer discover them when we have a Contract for Purchase and Sale accepted on the property. The benefit is that we can address those potential deal killers or high return investment repairs and provide the buyer with a clean bill of health on the home, which is a great pre-emptive negotiation strategy. Contrast this with having a buyer trying to re-negotiate the contract because of those inspection findings (and usually significantly over estimating repair costs in my experience). Market research shows that we can help home-sellers save 2 to 4% in repair costs versus price and we strive to help our clients keep more money in their pocket wherever possible. A home with a professional pre-inspection has a higher perceived value and lowers costs for the buyer, as they do not have to pay for their own inspection.

The home inspector did identify some issues in Pat and Grace's home, namely a deck without proper railing and a natural gas line leak. We utilized the services of our contractor and a plumber to rectify these issues. When we did receive the Contract for Purchase and Sale, the buyer did not see the need to obtain his own inspection, as we had made the professional pre-inspection available. Furthermore, since we had completed work on the identified issues, the pre-inspection essentially gave the home a clean bill of health and there was no basis in which the buyer could attempt to renegotiate the contract.

4. Professional Photography
In this day and age of digital connectivity, 92% of buyers search for homes online. As such, it is imperative that we have an effective online strategy. The biggest part of this is having a large number of high quality photos available online. Potential buyers are qualifying or disqualifying which homes to visit based on what they see online. I see far too many homes online which have subpar photos, and

in a lot of cases, not very many photos. Unfortunately, these real estate agents do not even realize that they are handicapping their seller clients. We employ a professional photographer to film all of our clients' homes. They utilize proper angles, lighting and a high definition camera. We also get our photographer to produce 360 degree virtual tours; when potential buyers are house hunting online, they literally feel like they are in the home looking around and can see how the house is laid out, the flow of rooms, etc. An important item to note is that a lot of our strategies tie together. For example, our stager consciously provides staging recommendations based on the effect they will have on the photos.

Pat and Grace were amazed at the difference in the quality of the photos our photographer took in comparison to the ones the other agent had previously taken. The professional photography, in conjunction with the staging which was done, resulted in their home appearing bright, spacious and inviting. This drove up the demand on Pat and Grace's home and a steady stream of buyers through their door.

5. Professional Copywriting

As important as professional photography is to visually attract and appeal to potential buyers, the written word holds more power over a buyer's emotion. Subpar ad copy does nothing to excite a potential buyer or capture their interest. That is why we utilize professional copywriting on all of our advertisements and property-listing descriptions. Effective ad copy can be used to personally target potential buyers and push their emotional hot buttons. For example, which sounds better? "Large maple kitchen with granite counters and island" or "This large maple kitchen features beautiful granite counter tops and plenty of room, including a large island, for preparing family meals." Many real estate agents just list features of homes; what the buyers really want to know is what are the benefits of the home to them. Another hallmark of effective ad copy is an effective call–to-action.

Most real estate ads and listings that I see, do not include a call-to-action. Effectively written ad copy includes a strong call-to-action. What do you want the potential buyers to do next? Call on the property to schedule a time to view it? Attend a weekend open house?

Pat and Grace's previous real estate agent specified features in short three to five-word sentences. We used professional copywriting which spelled out benefits to potential buyers reading the ads, triggered emotional hot buttons as well as an effective call-to-action. The result was a huge difference in the number of potential buyers looking at their home in comparison to the activity they experienced with their prior real estate agent.

6. Home Warranty
We have found that at any price range, providing Home Warranty coverage is extremely beneficial. The Home Warranty that we provide protects potential buyers by giving them a one-year coverage after they take ownership of the home. The Home Warranty covers major mechanical systems, such as plumbing, heating, cooling and appliances for the buyer. We find that providing Home Warranty aids in justifying the price of the property for the buyer and allows our clients' homes to sell faster and for more money.

Coupled with the pre-inspection, the Home Warranty gave Pat and Grace's buyer confidence to proceed with the purchase of the home and eliminated any potential doubt he may have had about purchasing it. It was just another level of protection that added to his comfort with the physical condition of the property.

7. Certified W.I.S.E. Buy
The Certified W.I.S.E. Buy designation is the ultimate way that we can help differentiate our client's home. W.I.S.E. stands for Warranty, Inspection (pre-inspection), Staging and Evaluation by appraiser. Just like a certified pre-owned car, we find that the Certified W.I.S.E. Buy designation

helps our clients' homes sell for a higher price, in a quicker time frame, and makes the buyer feel more comfortable and at ease with the home purchase compared to other similar properties for sale in the market place – ones which do not have the same benefits and protections in place, not to mention the assurance that the value is there in the property as the appraisal verifies.

Again, Pat and Grace's buyer had the utmost confidence that they were purchasing a sound home in great condition and that the price was justified by a credible third party.

The results delighted Pat and Grace. We generated 10 potential buyer appointments which resulted in having their home sold within 27 days, which allowed them to make their move well before trying to contend with maintaining their large property over another winter.

About Michael

Michael Kinar helps his clients sell their homes in a timely manner for the best price possible. Being raised on the family farm, Michael brings a strong work ethic to the real estate business. Michael embarked on his real estate career in 1999 and soon established himself as a top producing agent.

As he was fine tuning his home buying and selling process and systems, Michael realized that there was a lot more value and additional services that he and his real estate team could offer to their clients. Not wanting to have any restraints imposed on his vision, Michael left the real estate brokerage he was working at and formed his own company, Expert Advisor Realty. His goal is to continue providing the best client-experience possible alongside his team of Expert Advisors, by always putting the client and their needs first.

Michael is a proud member of the National Association of Expert Advisors, which has the vision to revolutionize the way consumers buy and sell real estate by providing the highest standards in specialized knowledge, skills training and advisory counsel to the highest class of real estate agents. Through the National Association of Expert Advisors, Michael has obtained designations as a Certified Home Selling Advisor as well as Certified Home Buying Advisor. He has been recognized as a Top 500 Real Estate Marketer and has been quoted in *The Star Phoenix* newspaper as well as on the Newstalk 650 radio station.

You can connect with Michael at:
michael@expertadvisorrealty.com
www.twitter.com/MichaelKinar
www.facebook.com/expertadvisorrealty